D0760290

PERSONAL GROWTH

AND

CREATIVITY

By the same Author:

Homoeopathic Medicine (Thorsons)

The Homoeopathic Treatment of Emotional Illness (Thorsons)

A Woman's Guide to Homoeopathy (Thorsons)

Understanding Homoeopathy (Insight)

An Encyclopaedia of Homoeopathy (Insight)

The Principles, Art and Practise of Homoeopathy (Insight)

Emotional Health (Insight)

PERSONAL GROWTH

AND

CREATIVITY

Dr Trevor Smith

Insight Editions

WORTHING. Sussex
ISBN O 946670 08 0
1986

First published 1986

© Trevor Smith 1986

British Library Cataloguing in Publication Data

Smith, Trevor, *1934-*
  Personal growth and creativity.
  1. Self-realization
  I. Title
  158'.1   BF637.S4

This book is sold subject to the condition that it shall not, by way or trade or otherwise, be lent, hired out or otherwise circulated without the publisher's prior consent in any form of binding or cover other that in which it is published and without a similar condition including this condition being imposed on the subsequent purchaser.

ISBN 0 946670 08 0

WARNING

The contents of this volume are for general interest only and individual persons should always consult their medical adviser about a particular problem or before stopping or changing an existing treatment.

Printed and bound in Great Britain by
Biddles Ltd, Guildford and King's Lynn

Contents

Recommendations to the Reader

If you have a known specific area of problem or blockage to creative expression, refer first to the section which deals with it. Use the index or the list of contents to find the relevant chapter.

Having read the appropriate section, study, develop and practise the recommended exercises daily. If there seems to be little change or outcome, practise the recommendations up to three times daily. Use the listed techniques and exercises as guidelines only but develop and use your own individual specific exercises for your particular problem, practise your own exercises, extend and develop them and practise daily.

Read through the whole book at least once to gain an overview of any problems and to stimulate new ideas. In general I recommend reading the whole book at least once a week until there is change.

Make your exercises practical, daring and imaginative. Don't give yourself a deadline for change as this is counter-productive and creates negative pressures rather than freeing positive factors.

Preface

The Paradox of Change (The Process of Creativity)

1. The Blocks

The problem, the fixed, the attached, the explicable, the predictable, the inevitable, the inflexible, the static, the non-creative, the impossible, the hopeless, the despair, the frustration, the dis-ease, the dissatisfaction, the lonely, the isolated, the being stuck, the certainty, the knowing, the logical, the definable, the fragmented, the chaotic, the unrelated, the irresolvable, the holding-in, the verbal, the conscious, the narrow, the confined, the strict.

2 The Paradox
(On two mountain peaks at the same time)

The double, the coincidence, the mysterious, the split, the meeting, the movement, the relationship, the link, the illogical, the breakthrough, the non-verbal, the surprise, the hope, the not-knowing, the unpredictable, the dissolution, the change, the illumination, the insight, the enlightenment, the perception, the opening, the inspiration, the indefinable, the inexplicable, the intermediate, the timeless, the imaginative, the no-boundaries, the overall, the sense of ease, sense of wonder, the uncertainty, the sense of awe, the gate, the opening, the pathway.

3. The Insight
(Quantum leap)

The creative, the new, the outcome, the endeavour, the artistic, the movement, the change, the intuitive, the freed, the unattached, the beginning, the consequence, the fluid, the shift, the happening, the growth, the resolution, the possible, the development, the idea, the unconscious, the spontaneous, the dance of ideas, the lightness, the space, the time, the shape, the form, the line, the awakening, the open, the wide, the available, the possible, the running, the light, the breakthrough.

Introductory
Overview

The following chapters aim to stimulate a practical insight into the major mental processes which directly influence original and inventive thinking. The book aims also to assist in the understanding and resolution of the common blocks which limit and lessen imaginative thought and explorative action in everyday life and problem-solving.

Every definition of creativity tends to be inadequate and unsatisfactory because it is quite impossible adequately to encompass such a fundamental dynamic process within the narrow confines and syntax of words. Essentially creativity is the process of innovation, change, originality and adjustment with the emphasis on new openings, outcome and new awareness within an area previously limited. Creativity seeks to find other ways, solutions and alternatives to problems and difficulties which impose their own answers and limits upon us – because we only perceive them within narrow boundaries and as a familiar presentation package.

There has always been confusion and difficulty concerning the creative process. Over the years it has increasingy been seen as something complex and mysterious, rare and unattainable for the majority, a gift of genius only given to the privileged few.

In reality, creativity is none of these things and far less complex. It is neither an intellectual nor a theoretical process, but a much more simple expression of curiosity and exploration, present in every healthy child and adult. It encompasses the ability to perceive, alter, change and to adapt in a situation of challenge in a whole variety of ways, solutions and viewpoints. Also to tolerate change and new solutions at a time of special need with new viewpoints and approaches. The creative approach imports new ideas and new energy into a previously stagnant area, re-arranging ideas, understanding and making links and associations in a way not previously perceived or thought of.

Most thinking is routine and limited by rigid or familiar patterns of assumption and fixed ideas. Change or challenge are seen and treated by identical attitudes and approach, whatever the situation and however different from a previous one. The underlying aim is to impose the same style and approach on each problem, irrespective of its particular characteristics, uniqueness and character. In this way the unconscious mind attempts to make it familiar and controllable, like an already known, established situation, rather than one which is new and requires a different approach, understanding and resolution. Creativity is always the natural expression of healthy inner psychological processes with ideas, viewpoints, approach and understanding which are a reflection of the individual at that stage in their development, experience, maturity and sensitivity. In this way, creativity reflects the ability to break-down and resolve established patterns and assumptions in a new way rather than imposing artificial solutions of convenience upon them or preserving them in limbo. By looking at the essentials and basic elements of each situation, rigid assumption-patterns can be overcome by a more overall individual approach – one which allows the trees to be seen as well as the wood, the component facts and ideas as well as the totality.

Because creativity is basically about change, it is also about life. Imagination is the conscious expression of creativity in thought form, by innovation, inventiveness and originality, however seemingly impracticable the outcome at the time. Most would agree that life should be a continuing challenge and encounter, each thought expressing in some way, an exciting adventure, with a willingness to explore, reappraise beliefs and established positions. There are no absolutes in life and no constants, except those of our own making. Science itself is in a state of flux, changed, doubled and re-written every five to seven years, yet science is also the nearest thing we have to absolutes.

In general, creative ideas are break-through ideas, which pierce the barrier of habit, cliché, patterns and conformity, liberating new and previously unperceived, unavailable links, associations and implications.

In this way, it also liberates quite fundamental aspects of the individual, who to some degree becomes psychologically renewed or re-located by each creative experience and insight. This re-location of self happens to some extent with every creative experience and insight, however brief, both within a specific problem area as also in a more generalised, yet personal way. Whenever a problem area is perceived differently, with new insights and perspectives, there is also a shift in personal depths and understanding with changes in overall awareness and sensitivity. In this way creativity is a liberating process at a personal level as well as at the level of blockage or impasse. Creative problem-solving and a shift in personal sensitivity and awareness are both closely interlinked and sometimes it is difficult to say which preceded the other.

Creativity relates to inventiveness and discovery at some level, but it does not necessarily imply a major breakthrough of genius or exceptional talent. There is often a new yet straightforward, simple expression or approach to a commonplace situation, like decorating a room, planning a garden or experimenting with a meal. It can occur in the kitchen, as much in the studio or laboratory, with new and better solutions, to trimming a hedge, sewing a hem, or making a sauce, and any of these may be just as original and creative as a finding in the scientific field. Although creativity is only rarely the outcome of exceptional talent, it is nearly always associated with passionate interest, hard-work, persistence and involvement over a period of weeks or months, frequently at quite a conscious level. A breakthrough comes suddenly as a surprise, largely because of the unconscious processes involved and the self-limiting fixed attempts to change a situation according to previous ideas and concepts.

In general, when we are creative, we are also more open and 'authentic', more ourselves and spontaneous as people. Each new, unknown, challenging situation stimulates a wider, deeper response and awareness, which expands the individual as it allows broader and a greater variety of limits and associations to occur. Because the mind does not work in isolation, but only in tandem with the whole person, as each problem is expanded, so too is the individual. Everyone has creative potential, but after childhood, few use it. Originality becomes blocked by habit, fear and education as well as by social upbringing and lack of encouragement for anything other than the conforming. We are taught to imitate, rather than to innovate or be different, to produce results and answers, not to think or synthesise. Our present, largely rigid icational system trains perception and derstanding along narrow formal lines, with tle time or sympathy for broader alternative, iallenging considerations, in case they bring the whole approach and system into question. Because of the examination system, most children are quickly programmed into established habits and patterns in school, with thought-expanding programmes kept minimal and the emphasis on syllabus and a routine to problem solving. Such patterns and approaches are difficult to break in later life. Awareness of alternative perceptions and possibilities to a difficulty or challenge are rarely rewarded or encouraged, except in a few highly individual exceptional cases, because the examination system tests facts and figures, along narrow well-defined channels, emphasising routine answers. Little sympathy is given to 'unconventional' thinking or unconscious processing, unless it is organised, logical and coherent, and this is extremely rare in the early stages of creative insight as new links are largely unconscious and the processes which lead to intuition and new thinking are not easily explainable in conventional terms.

Initially all life is a process of stimulation, awareness and adjustment. New experiences and feelings are linked and related to others, with both instinctual and unconscious processes available in an expanding growing awareness which allows a broad combination of responses so that new learning, exploration and growth can occur. From the earliest weeks of life, there is a combination of exploration, change, renewal and association at both physical and psychological levels, with a varied expression of stimulation and responses available for each occasion, as natural awareness and flexible understanding.

From the first moments of sucking at the teat or nipple, adjustment and innovation are needed, according to the feel, size, firmness and pressures needed to control the flow of milk. Such simple feeding-contacts differ with each mother-child relationship in some way, reflecting individual needs and temperament. The ability to communicate, adjust, alter, create and innovate is as basic to the young baby as the inborn sucking reflex and develops from it. To ensure an adequate supply of warmth, holding and nutritional needs, rapid learning and adaptation are required to communicate need, feeling, hunger and pain, love and responsiveness. At about the same time, the infant also becomes aware of the effects of its own sounds and noises, reactions from the mother, her sounds, gestures and a whole new spectrum of rewards and satisfactions, which brings satisfactions as well as limitations and frustrating drawbacks.

After a few short weeks or months of liquid food, the process of weaning or severance begins, also bringing a new challenge to learning and experience. There is a sense of loss and deprivation, as well as the introduction to a whole new world of foods, tastes, consistencies, temperatures and satisfactions. All of these lead to a new sense of expanding awareness, interest and perceptual development. As reality boundaries are extended by each different and new experience, so too maturation of the individual evolves with new areas of demand and interest as each new contact leads to challenge, adjustment and stimulation to originality.

Challenge and its resolution brings with it deep and important psychological satisfactions and securities as each step mastered is a stepping-stone to maturity, drive and confidence to explore and innovate in ever increasing areas. New perceptions and awareness develop, opening up experience, contact and self-expression, with the past, eventually less of a security haven to be rushed back to in times of fear and threat as personal ego strengths and confidence expand and grow. These primary infant growth steps lead to a series of fascinating challenges, each to be explored and creatively resolved.

Throughout early healthy development, every step is both creative and original as the child strains to meet and respond to each new stimulus which an evolving development is constantly evoking.

The child can now for the first time begin to separate-out phantasy wishes from reality frustrations and gratifications and to differentiate self from others. During this period of maximum growth and change, the experience of feed-back and response from others is fundamental for confidence, individuality and experimentation to occur. Some wind, colic and pain are inevitable during these early months of every child's development and present both as frustration as well as a challenge to communication in order to bring relief. But each child develops its own highly individual and usually efficient patterns of self-expression for need and want, comfort and satisfaction so that the mother or mother-figure is left in no doubt as to the true feelings and wants of her child, the meaning of each varied expression. A highly original communications system is quickly evolved and expanded, largely of a non-verbal nature which integrates and expands developing sounds and gestures into vocal and verbal expressions of need and want, making for an effective mother-child communication and relationship which is the basis for future creativeness.

Growth proceeds by a series of external changes as physical maturation takes place. Innovation and adjustment expand according to the needs of each situation, sensitivity of the mother and the temperament and personality of the child. To some extent, these early contacts and innovations dominate all later originality, experimentation and creative endeavour. Where they have been positive and appreciated during childhood, rewarded by encouragement and support they are likely to be carried on into later adult life as a readiness to innovate and flexibility to meet challenges throughout life. Where the early innovation attempts were severely trimmed, threatened, unsatisfactory or made to feel a source of criticism, pain or disapproval, then in later life they are likely to be less active. The adult is more subdued, partial and inhibited with some infantile fear never far removed from each creative endeavour and an undermining feature to spontaneity, exposure and taking a chance in a new area or association of ideas.

Change is a constant necessity for health and growth at every level. In order for growth to occur there must be break-down and alteration, movement in some form, however apparently useless, negative and destructive at the time. This is crucial: physiologically, to avoid excretion and detoxication products being retained, and psychologically to ensure confidence and the build-up of new experience. Every child will at some time break, throw-out, reject some of its toys as part of experimentation and play. Adults too need to do this throughout life, in order to break-through boundaries of perfection, certainty and restraint which social upbringing tries to impose. If not, there is a paralysing inertia to creative efforts as a result. Newness also brings a similar paralysing effect, like the artist's blank canvas before there is a line or wash upon it.

New challenges to adaptation and survival, understanding and relationships occur throughout life, both at home and in school, in the office or on the sports field. Learning a new skill, movement or control, like balancing a bicycle or driving a car, require a new and novel approach, exposure and test of confidence, beyond simple instinctual patterns of response and conditioned learning.

Much of the lack of creative ability in our present society systems stems from an educational system and upbringing, which wrongly emphasises 'correct' results and repetitive learning with only lip service paid to the individual approach, to new ideas, concepts or innovation. Internal or psychological blocks add to the social, educational and cultural barriers and either completely stem the flow of originality or severely limit it.

Attempts to deny creativity and change, are also attempts to deny life and individuality itself. Although these external blocks do not prevent creativity, they can deviate its outlets and limit available channels of expression into more contrived and often anti-social modes of expression.

Blockage at more internal psychological levels leads to neurosis as its alternative creative expression bound by all the limitations of rigidity, repetition, omnipotence and emotional certainty imposed upon it.

Creative drive is fundamental to *homo sapiens*, and however much in doubt, anguish, or grief-stricken, there are still many ways and opportunities to be new, individual and different, despite attempts by a sick or neurotic ego to bridle and control innovation and change. Nothing in life is ever quite static, without some movement, however imperceptible. The most inorganic mineral expressions of nature have their tides, changes and seasons of difference in energy flows, because they too are in a constant state of change, developmental flux, evolution and maturation.

The creative individual approach accepts an impasse as part of challenge, the experience of existence and being, without panic, able to stay within both self and situation. Some chaos and disorder are common but there should be no opting for a premature tidying-up just to remove the problem without an individual solution. In this way, more time is made available for a broader, more imaginative approach. Although unable to respond or resolve a problem immediately, the creative person is prepared to forgo the satisfactions of immediate answers in favour of delayed, more meaningful solutions allowing new links and associations, not previously obvious. In this way, even where there is stress-pressure, new learning and insight-links can still occur.

When a creative approach is given time to expand and mature, the individual does not lose confidence, nor is thrown-off course, by a problem which does not offer immediate solutions. Because every situation must evolve and change without exception, an alternative creative approach can always emerge, given sufficient time, to reveal 'other' solutions, once the decision to defer the quick answer has been decided upon.

An organisation as complex as the human mind is constantly inter-relating perceptual, psychological, intellectual and social attitudes, but with only one direction for meaningful expression, and that is outwards, towards others. Growth, contact, experience are the main ways that change, new ideas, perceptions and insights can be expressed. Withdrawal, denial, blockage and suppression are rarely possible for more than a limited period without undermining health. We just cannot sustain narrow attitudes and patterns of self-interest, yet develop and grow at the same time. The most controlled, limited, psychological state cannot restrict all change and movement however. Some innovation and change always take place, however much controls are imposed and certainties applied.

Change and variety are a major feature of every healthy life and innovation with development an intrinsic part of maturation. The first sign of creative development may be awareness and an admission of being blocked, psychologically stagnant in certain areas, the overwhelming need for change. Such insight may be clearly followed by a shift in basic attitudes, drives and aims with changes in well-established patterns. It sometimes occurs after a loss, period of grief or deep and significant encounter. When we are original in thinking and attitude, we also replenish ourselves and are in balance. Creativity is innovation and without it there is illness, discomfort, malaise, eventually psychological or physical disease.

When we are fully ourselves, we are naturally original because there is a freedom of ideas and associations, fun, spontaneity and play which frees movement and openness. Creative thought is being prepared for each new situation and development, having the courage to throw out reassuring patterns for new, more relevant and rewarding ones.

Creativity harmonises with the person as a totality so that a more sensitive, expanded state of mind and individuality develops.

Health always reflects change and renewal as well as growth and elimination at physical and psychological levels. The creative approach to life is essentially the individual one, with a willingness to explore, more open to each situation as it *is*, rather than as we would like it to be.

The creative response is outward and other-directed, with a full expression of feelings and associations, rather than a defensive partial one. Such encounters, change and re-orientate to some degree providing a re-appraisal of directions and assumptions, supporting growth and change because every aspect of the self is involved in some way as part of the total contact and involvement. A well-written, rhythmic poem is not just an intellectual exercise, but also a deep psychological and spiritual encounter within the self. Whatever the outside stresses and pressures, when we are creative, we are also less dependent upon patterns and recipe-thinking of constraint, limit and habit. This gives the greatest independence and more balanced perspectives.

In this way, growth and creativeness are inseparable from individuality. When we are in balance and ourselves, natural, spontaneous, we are in an optimum position to see things as they are, to respond spontaneously, to make new links and perspectives. At such times, an uncertain situation, with no obvious immediate solutions, can be changed into an exciting potential one, be more tolerated and less of a threat. Because it has potential, it can also evolve into other shapes, forms and situations, develop a new clarity because of its intrinsic potential for change however seemingly chaotic in the present. In this way there is greater tolerance and a more overall perspective so that a different evolving outcome is possible.

The healthy integrated person is neither psychologically fragmented nor in bits and pieces in terms of identity. In this way, he or she is able to think more broadly and widely, to be more daring in imaginative thinking and concepts, viewpoints and planning, because they can 'let go' of themselves and really experience each situation to a maximum, as a reality as well as at a phantasy level. In illness there is more of a self-protective, self-orientated approach to life and challenge which narrows and to some extent dominates understanding, spontaneity and thinking, leading to a limited, controlled pattern of response.

When man ceases to create, he is sick because the essential internal processes of renewal, openness and replenishment are blocked.

External creativity reflects internal creativity, dynamic change and balance. Illness occurs when the natural innovative processes become blocked, deviated by fear and negative certainty, causing diminished patterns of vitality and resistance which undermine individuality and encourage physical disequilibrium. In this way, the whole creative process of life becomes blocked by fixed, rigid uncreative patterns which limit imaginative thought and innovative perception.

Background, social patterns and upbringing all impose their own particular intrinsic patterns as to how we receive, interpret and respond to information and contact. Too often a psychological mould or stamp is imposed upon all behaviour and understanding which limits new thinking, spontaneity of association and response. The truly creative position occurs where there is freedom and independence from all fixed psychological assumptions and rigid mental structures. In order for creativeness to develop there has to be a significant shift and a freeing of habitual confining attitudes of the past which prevent changes in perception and response from occurring and new view-points developing.

At some time, everyone needs to admit a breakthrough and a letting-go of their established patterns of passivity and inertia. Once the break has been made, they can express themselves more openly, able to consider alternatives with a more expanded awareness leading to greater personal growth. We are as we perceive, see and understand. When we see only in terms of set limits, fixed assumptions, defined areas and patterns, this also reflects fixed internal limits and inner patterns.

A static mind gives rise to sickness and ill-health, because of constricted attitudes which inevitably create inertia and paralysis. Where the mind is more dynamic and flexible, open to changing experience, then personal growth naturally occurs. Once a creative link is made, there is an experience of relief and freedom because the individual is at that moment less dominated by past, controlling, fixed assumptions. Each time a creative link is made, it gives a satisfaction in depth because an opening has been made within formerly closed areas of the self. This leads to a greater sense of wholeness, freedom from restriction, relief at being integrated and a sense of being at one with existence and totality.

Holding on to a problem area can sometimes be as important as letting go, especially where in the past, poor controls have led to excessive emotional reactions, or attempts to impose infantile controls. A quieter, less dramatic approach to a particular problem area was not possible at the time and only a more overall creative approach with a broader viewpoint, leads to a more 'laid back' approach. But each dynamic approach varies with the individual and particular situation of the time.

Because no two people are ever quite alike, and no solution totally static, there is an infinite variety of original approaches possible to every situation. These may be either formal and traditional or more radical and different. The number of new ideas, variations and perceptions possible is not usually limited by the form of presentation of a problem unless it is part of an imposed pattern that cannot be broken for emotional and neurotic reasons.

There are no absolutes to life and every boundary is at least potentially permeable and alterable, open to change and expansion, whether organic or inorganic. Even that first and most familiar equation of $2+2=4$ is about an expanding,contracting dynamic and largely symbolic 2, rather than an absolute or static duality, inert with no shift or movement occurring within it. Like everything in life, even the symbolic 2 is changing and evolving, if not it is unreal and inexact. We are however in general far too ready only to think in terms of absolutes and unchangeables, rather than the more rewarding dynamic concepts.

The reality is that even the most ordinary, seemingly static household glass tumbler is not only expanding and contracting with atmospheric changes, but changing and maturing internally by the slow processes of crystallisation, becoming opaque or devitrified according to the temperature and the impurities present.

The absolute and unchanging concept is a barrier to all creative thinking because nothing in nature is static and still. Only the dynamic changing exists in life, allowing a broader imaginative approach so that at one moment $2+2=4+$ and at another $2+2=4$ –. Like definitions, standards and absolutes are highly suspect, confining, relative considerations which block or limit original thinking because they impose contrived unreal assumptions upon thinking, limiting new perspectives and idea-relationships by artificial or repetitive barriers.

But neither neurotic emotion nor psychological illness blocks creativity, they only change its external form. The works of some of our greatest artists have clearly shown this. Creativity at times of extreme emotion, strain, breakdown or turmoil often has a flat, repetitive note to it, sometimes a recurring theme or bizarre component, a sense of concreteness which need not distract from its merit, originality and innovation.

The 'removal' of neurosis by psychoanalysis does not diminish creativity either because creative innovation and new thinking are not dependent upon neurosis for their drive and motivation. But analysis cannot guarantee either that creativity will occur when the individual is 'freed' from neurotic blocks, although creative achievement is more likely.

Most neurosis is a constant repetition of self-orientated patterns, ways of behaviour and interpretation of phenomena, rather than new, daring, different thinking which is basic to innovation, change, alternative solutions and new ideas.

Because neurosis always aims to control self and others, rather than to allow one to experience life as it is and happens, this leads to the typical symptoms of boredom, frustration, depression and sense of inadequacy. Failure of spontaneity and self-expression leads to feelings of non-existence, retention and blockage so that each new experience and encounter is taken at half-throttle, pre-judged and never fully enjoyed or participated. The internal emotional stasis that develops eventually leads to blocked basic drives and psychological expressions, with physical processes also undermined as the processes of change, renewal and replenishment are kept controlled and minimal at every level.

The purpose of life is to experience and give form and shape to our personal inspirational self and deity, however we conceive of them and whatever words we use to describe them. The inspirational self is clearly evidenced in the creativity and vision – not only of the great architects and cathedral builders, but by every aspect of real artistic expression and thinking, when man is in tune with his ultimates.

However advanced the insights and knowledge into scientific, technological, medical and psychological processes, life still remains a mystery, and it is this indefinable aspect which gives much of the thrust towards original achievement. When the inspirational ultimate is expressed by original and creative innovation we are also closest to our own mystery and origins.

Chapter one

Physical Blocks to Creativity

Physical well-being is just as important as psychological balance in maintaining health and both play a key role in preserving it. A creative approach to life can occur under the most appalling physical pressures, sometimes because of them rather than in spite of the limitations. But this tends to be the exception rather than the rule and in most situations, where there is a physical illness or limitation, creativity is reduced – either directly from the physical cause or because of anxiety concerning it. For the majority, a physical limitation, unless burned-out and chronic, is not the ideal for innovation and 'break-through' to occur. Beethoven was creative in spite of the severe limitations of his deafness. Lautrec painted brilliantly despite the problems of his size and appearance. For the majority, physical pain and pressure undermine creative drive and impulse rather than acting as a trigger to its realisation. Chronic, debilitating states and long-standing physical illness problems also limit creativity because of negative attitudes to the problem in a repetitive, circular way, as much as the limitations of the actual problem.

Creative self-expression to problem solving in some cases is limited by pain or fear, as expansive attitudes are blocked by physical investigation and treatment, fear of dying and a whole variety of unknowns, but always depending upon the individual psychological health as well as the amount of clarification and information given. Often imaginative, open attitudes are diminished by depression and failure to realise that every physical problem can be turned to an advantage, as long as the underlying attitudes are right and a sense of humour and balance are maintained. Ill health is always the outcome of blockage to resistance and to the free-flow of vitality and drainage at some level. Blocks to the flow of ideas, energy, vitality and curiosity are as much part of illness as major aspects of creative drive and its fulfilment.

Physical causes, especially chronic or 'difficult' problems, are often inseparable from the psychological blocks and commonly associated with feelings of fear, futility and hopelessness because they are felt to be incurable and depressing. The real danger of a physical condition is that it 'takes over' the personality, leading to impoverishment of ideas and originality or a sense of passivity and acceptance which leads to jaded creative efforts and 'not having to bother'.

A 55 year old teacher and sensitive poet became completely undermined of all creative drive and inspiration because of an acute rheumatic condition which severely limited mobility and ease of movement. He ceased working and writing and became preoccupied with his various doctors, drugs, treatments and therapies, like a possessive infant. The wife colluded to the extent of taking early retirement to nurse him, so that she too lost her own creative drive as part of their joint involvement with his 'problem'. Both their creative energies became centred and lost within the problem of rehabilitating and nursing him. Deeper dissatisfactions and problems in other areas were never fully brought out into the open or discussed, although these could have been a source of possible creative thinking and energy for them both. Creativity became the scapegoat for their collusive denials and a chronic, unresolvable condition developed for both as an outcome of the blockage.

Psychosomatic illness is the physical expression of the emotional, with psychological energy diverted into non-emotional areas of outlet and expression. It is always undermining and tends to limit creative living. Chronic problems of the skin, mucosa or internal organs, develop from not creatively confronting and resolving a psychological challenge as it occurs. In general there is lack of awareness and insight as to the meaning and origins of diverted emotional threads, and this is a major cause of problems becoming chronic.

However limiting the psychosomatic problem, the 'pay off' is that pressures and demands are felt to be temporarily lifted or made more controllable by a condition or demand with a 'real' and tangible reality. The problems tend to be powerful, dramatic and sudden, avoiding the need to do anything or to make innovation or change, because they take priority over all other considerations at the time. Such is their power and influence. There is felt to be more tolerance, sympathy and acceptance by others, which is a powerful factor in maintaining them. Such symptoms can often be self-destructive, particularly asthma or colitis, but because at the same time they are powerful weapons psychologically to control others, they are constantly repeated and each crisis usually further limits creative expressions and drive.

Where a physical channel becomes blocked, from either physical or psychological reasons, rather than acting as an outlet for expression and individuality, a chronic situation may develop which further limits new ideas and thinking. Flexible, imaginative thinking is lost or lessened by a chronic, physically demoralising problem, especially when diminished functioning and vitality already causes impairment of movement and expression.

Chronic physical problems are often the end-result of blocked creative drive, which over a period has slowly led to devitalised physical and psychological energy flows. This eventually leads to physical degeneration and limitation as much as with innovative thought, experimentation and action.

A 45 year old executive with a chronic low back problem for several years had applied for a post as a company financial director. Because of pain, he cancelled the interviews, although the recurrence had only been present for a short time. In this way he was able to avoid the necessity of making a major change, which had been put off over several years. He avoided looking at his reasons for being stuck in a job with inadequate prospects as much as why he was immobilised in the low back region.

When physical channels are blocked, rather than an outlet for functioning and expression, a chronic situation develops of a physical or psychological nature. New challenging responses may be impossible because of the symptoms, aggravated by new demand for energy expression. Flexible imaginative thinking is lost or lessened by chronic problems, especially where functioning and vitality are impaired with freedom of mobility and expression. Where spontaneity is undermined, so too is health reduced and limited, including the creative health of the individual.

Mobility and Movement Blockages to Creativity.

Joint and skeletal structures not only support the whole body but also provide key mobility and encounter function, permitting changes in time and space, movement, position and posture. This is always one of the commonest areas where rigidity, immobility and limitation occur. Especially common are arthritis, rheumatism, cramp, spasm, frozen shoulder, lumbago, tennis elbow and writers cramp. All of these limit, because they give a physical label to an area of non-functioning, expressing unconscious attempts to limit movement, meeting, new experience, new relationships, new encounters. Diets, drugs, treatment, investigations and therapy, generally focus emphasis on the externals and the physical rather than the true causes.

Voco-Laryngeal Blockages to Creativity.

These may be physical in origin as from a polyp or paralysed or infected chord or psychological or with hysterical paralysis. There are many chronic as well as acute problems of the pharynx, throat, nose and upper respiratory tract in general including the chronic allergies as hay fever and sinusitis. All of these block individual expression and limit relationships and energy in general and a free imaginative approach to life. The physical limitations cause psychological limitations, blocking creative as well as the drainage pathways. Chronic cough or chronic hoarseness, with a whispering speech, chronic discomfort and aching undermines drive and innovative energy because much of it is sucked away into situations of chronic blockage.

Visual-Receptive Blockages to Creativity.

These include problems of diminished vision and visual accommodation. Infection, allergy, irritation, degenerative problems, duct blockage and pressure build-up in the ocular organ are some of the other problems which make for visual uncertainty and lack of clarity. None of the above is an absolute block to creativity as the work of many blind musicians and therapists has demonstrated over the years. But chronic anxiety, uncertainty about diagnosis, fear of blindness, are blocks to creativity rather than a challenge or stimulus to it. Frustration and uncertainty tends to lessen new thinking, ideas and channels of origination, rather than leading to their positive development. Others may be both supportive as well as discouraging, limiting in their attitudes, because of their fears and the demands that involvement and caring are felt to bring.

A physical problem *can* be a stimulus to overcoming a disability and a challenge, as shown by Douglas Bader, whose loss of limbs led him to even greater determination, creative drive and achievement. Equally a physical problem can be a powerful stimulus to passivity and defence against change, demoralising and taking over all healthy, outward-directed motivation, aims and thinking.

Chronic Alimentary Problems and Blockages to Creativity.

Where digestive channels are blocked, either psychologically or physically, with problems of ulceration, acidity, heartburn, spasm, haemorrhage, scar-tissue narrowing and pain, irritability or discomfort, there is imbalance, leading to exhaustion, weakness and general lack of drive and initiative. All of this undermines thinking, innovation and the energy to expand because of impaired energy absorption and release. Anaemia may further reduce the drive available for the expansion, exploration and follow-through of new ideas and associations.

Pelvic Blockage to Creativity.

These arise from a variety of reasons, especially trauma, infection, childbirth, or psychological causes. Fibroids, polyps and hernia with uterine, prostate and bladder problems are the commonest areas of dysfunction which undermine function and essential elimination. All vary considerable in type, severity, duration and degree. Often a surgical course is necessary or where there is an infection a course of antibiotics. Because they are painful and undermining, they drain energy, drive and direction until resolved. The pelvic area is a vital part of both elimination, reproduction and sexual functioning with many emotional associations and these further complicate the condition.

Pain, discomfort and anxiety about treatment or diagnosis all undermine confidence, especially where the flow of information is limited with regard to diagnosis and outcome. Chronic pelvic problems can be a major cause of diminished creativity which is difficult to resolve, depending upon the problem, cause and severity.

Allergic-sensitivity Blocks to Creativity.

With chronic allergic problems, discomfort and limitation are often severe. Typical symptoms and problems are mucosal congestion leading to swelling and discharge in any sensitized part of the body, causing swelling, discharge, pain, blockage and headache. Allergic reaction to food substances, usually involve their protein components, and a common cause is sensitivity to dairy-foods, wheat, gluten, chocolate, sugar, animal-hair, house-dust, pollen and moulds. All may trigger-off a sensitivity-rejection response in an attempt to expel the allergic component from the body. Such reactions impair physical well-being as well as creativity. Some less well-known trigger factors are hormones and tenderisers in meat, colorants in pill capsules, shell-fish and antibiotics. Every allergic reaction tends to limit innovation because of a jaded sense of well-being. The individual feels below par and devitalised as well as demoralised by a stuffed-up chronic catarrhal condition, often with no particular season or time sequence to it. Typical swelling, burning pain, congestion and blockage cause irritability or depression, sometimes both, and act as a check to original thinking, patience and spontaneity. The commonest prescription is usually one of the anti-decongestant agents, which further limit alertness or cause drowsiness as congestion is reduced. The combination of a sedative effect from the drugs and the misery of the condition diminishes concentration, drive and overall effectiveness.

Non-specific Conditions as Blocks to Creativity

These include degenerative conditions and patterns of cellular disorganisation as occurs in certain growths, nervous diseases like Disseminated Sclerosis, Parkinsonism or hereditary problems as Huntingdon's Chorea. The causes are often unknown, or due to obscure viral infections, deficiency conditions or genetic reasons. The problems are chronic because they are of unknown causation and treatment tends to be non-specific and unsatisfactory. As they undermine the nervous system in some way, often with a progressive weakness, this also undermines body and mind and with them creativity.

Rigidity of attitude adds to any existing problems of fear, anxiety and additional strain. Each problem needs specific treatment where available and close consideration of underlying attitudes and psychological traits, especially where the condition has developed as part of an overall reaction to stress and strain or loss.

If we consider the physical changes that take place from birth onwards, the healthy child is either fully relaxed and asleep or full of energy, new learning and exploration, busy with games, mischief and fun. There is a contrasting balance between tone and movement, impulse and need. The healthy child lies easy and relaxed, once basic needs are satisfied, with a mixture of awareness, spontaneity, interest and vitality.

By the age of eight to ten, many children have already lost some of this ease, spontaneity and naturalness. There is often painful self-awareness, low self-esteem, shyness and self-consciousness, pressures, sometimes uncertainty or anxiety as a reaction to the combined pressures of education and upbringing. The teenager may be difficult to live with because they find themselves and others a problem to relate to, so that there is a return of compulsive infantile needs for sweet foods and mouth satisfactions – as a prop and reassurance.

By the early twenties, much of the softness of the child has often gone permanently, together with loss of drive, sometimes confusion about direction and identity. There is a seeking after media models of identity and ideals, rather than expanding personal experience, individuality, and intuitive awareness. By thirty, many are tired and jaded, both at work and in personal relationships. At forty, many already feel on the shelf and past it. By fifty the dynamic young child has changed into an insecure, rigid, tense shadow of being, media-dependent or dominated, grimly carrying on within limited boundaries of thinking and perception, with numerous no-go areas of control of his or her own making. Psychologically as well as physically stiff, awkward from obesity and impaired by limited psychological perceptions, vitality is already limited so that only a minimum of drive and energy is available for the new perceptions and the fresh understanding needed for creative drive.

The social addictions, alcohol, pills, tobacco and the media, stimulate the pursuit of unreal phantasy-ideals, rather than an expanded self-awareness. Too often religion, which could play a significant meaningful part in developing creative self-expression, is also used as a reassurance and a prop, rather than a stimulus to new depth thinking, imaginative awareness and caring. Television and video encourage passivity and uncreative spectator-attitudes. Fast food fosters the quick and the instant rather than an awareness of food as a more creative loving experience. The drive for the quick and the rapid puts emphasis also on symptom-relief only rather than underlying meaning with an urgency to suppress by synthetics, wonder-drugs and pills without insight or understanding into any personal roles or responsibility. All of this undermines awareness, identity, vitality and creative drive.

In general we seek to control and lessen frustrations and low self-esteem but without understanding it because of passivity which severely limits awareness and ability. Increasingly the emphasis is on the familiar and the known, rather than the development of new links, ideas and developments.

The media increasingly takes over time, initiative and drive as man becomes a pawn in a commercial exercise, rather than a participant in a wide variety of experiences. Originality, personal growth and sensitivity are the victims of the passivity which occurs.

As automation, early retirement and redundancy make more time available to re-consider directions, aims and priorities, there is a greater possibility than ever before of modifying former rigid or negative patterns. This allows each individual the real opportunity of significant new development, more open attitudes and perceptions as long as the change can be accepted and tolerated.

Creative drive and the re-alignment and discovery of alternative ideas and concepts are the natural expression of a balanced healthy mind. They are not necessarily related to either brilliance or talent. Turner's water colours have both power and impact, not because they are a work of talent, but because their spontaneity and creative energy can be clearly felt. Blake's drawings or a Moore sculpture give the opportunity momentarily to participate and share an enlightening experience and to sense their flow and movement which give a brief flash of relief and freedom from the man-made knots of pattern and conformity.

Once vital energy flows again, through a physical blockage or knot, there is renewed expression of drive and an opening of channels as the cells or organs concerned are re-established into health and functioning. Meditation and visualisation are some of the techniques used to facilitate physical un-blocking, but dreams, meaningful contact with others, stillness and closeness with nature are also effective in freeing blocked areas and liberating creative flow again.

Chapter two

Social-addictive Blocks to Creativity

Smoking.

Because tobacco impairs gaseous interchange at the delicate lung surface and impairs vital circulation, it also undermines health and energy release. Because it is a comfort habit which seeks to control and deny tension or discomfort, it appears relaxing, but smoking imposes a superficial limited brand of relaxation, strictly controlled through ritual, habit and patterns. This is often apparent when a situation of deprivation occurs for any reason, as with temporary unavailability, when severe anxiety and irritability quickly breaks through. Because smoking impairs well-being and health, it also impairs freedom and efficiency, especially where there are added physical problems such as asthma, bronchitis or emphysema. Creativity and flexibility are impaired because of the habit and like other addictions of a similar type it reinforces non-creative attitudes of rigidity, sameness, self-control and dependency as a thin defence against loss of control or anxiety.

Alcohol.

The drink habit of a glass in hand tends in moderation to encourage ease and relaxation in a social situation where there is a new contact with other people. At the same time, it is a cerebral poison, sedating and dulling awareness and imaginative thinking. Like all the social addictive habits, it is open to abuse, fine in moderation, but a danger in excess. Physical alterations to the stomach, liver, cerebral and cardiac circulatory tissues, are a clear proof of its toxic nature.

Changes begin in a minor insidious way, lessening fine sensitive awareness and creative innovation before more gross physical and psychological changes occur. In general, alcohol reinforces circular patterns of superficial, repetitive thinking which later lead on to depression.

Food.

Over-eating is one of the major social vices which impairs health and life-expectation. Excessive weight makes for a dull mind and body. Psychological problems including depression and low self-esteem add to the physical damage. Because it puts emphasis on eating and dieting as a way of life in an unimaginative compulsive fashion, it emphasises dependency and undermines independence of thinking or originality. There is a preoccupation with diet, weight and compulsive snacking. Its opposite, anorexia nervosa of young adults, is equally self-destructive. With body weight at critical even to danger levels, it also limits creative expression and achievement until the body weight and physiology has been put back into balance and the underlying psychological condition resolved.

Problems of allergy and food sensitivity tend to further limit health, awareness and well-being with a variety of chronic conditions that may defy all diagnosis and treatment. Because food addiction emphasises suppression, reassurance, comfort and 'gut' reactions, it also dulls sensitive-awareness.

Prescribed Pharmaceutic-Addictive Blockages to Creativity.

These include the regular use of synthetic drugs to suppress or block disagreeable symptoms, such as pain-killers or antacids which impair health and well-being as a side-effect of their action. In general, whatever drug is taken, none is without risk and all have some degree of side-effect, differing only in degree. Synthetic vitamin pills come into the same category, giving a temporary lift but when taken over prolonged periods cause imbalance and a tendency to be dependent on supplements rather than natural resources. Anti-depressants, anti-hypertensives, (blood pressure), anti-spasmodics (spasm), pills, tranquillisers, laxatives and aperients all limit and reduce health to some extent, because they reduce natural functioning. They may encourage dependency and the true underlying reasons for a problem developing. To the degree that they encourage denial and dependency, they also inhibit innovation.

Prohibited Pharmaceutic-Addictive Blocks to Creativity.

These include the hard and soft drugs which at present are being sold or taken illegally in every European city. Heroin, cocaine, L.S.D., marihuana, amphetamines, glues, fungoids and plants are included in the list, taken either by mouth, through the mucosa or by injection. There is an attempt to gain a respite from reality, an escape into a phantasised 'high' state of bliss, that rarely materialises. Any brief stimulation is at best short lived, quickly followed by a severe depressive 'low' or let down. Because they are illegal, this gives an added measure of excitement as well as encouraging anti-social acts to finance them. Because they are addictive, they encourage routine non-productive thought and usually uncreative phantasy-experiences. There is a widespread myth prevalent that such experiences are harmless and lead to a liberation-experience, widening of perceptions and insight with increased boundaries of awareness and creativity. This is wishful thinking however, encouraged by commercial interests. Only rarely does drug taking lead to a true creative break-through.

Drugs have been used to try to combat fatigue, depression and social or sexual barriers, but often they create the very problems they seek to overcome. Physical side effects include constipation, infection, impaired resistance, ulceration and collapse. Because addiction is an excessive attachment to one particular idea, solution or recipe, it tends to impose its own rules and interpretations of life and reality so that creative thought is ultimately limited, rather than open and expanded.

Chapter three

Social and Environmental Blocks to Creativity

Situational Factors.

In order for free-flowing thought and new associations to take place, the situation or room must be physically comfortable and well-positioned, in harmony with the needs of the individual and his or her temperament. A work or stimulus room which is too small gives a womb-like sense of enclosure as much as security and comfort and tends to limit new ideas and links occurring. Because small narrow rooms are felt to be constricting, they lead to more immature thought-patterns, related to infantile needs and association rather than explorative ones and innovation. A room which is large may help expand ideas, but if it is too big, the excess of space becomes an uncomfortable distraction until it is filled-in, given a boundary which is more comfortable. A basement work area may lead to a sense of being underground, with a cellar-like feeling of constriction. In general a higher, more elevated room is preferable, although an attic room can be airless and oppressive, too hot in summer, associated with feelings of constriction. An over-crowded room is always a distraction and limiting because of the lack of personal space. A large, open-plan office is sound economically but not creatively and there are often insufficient personal boundaries to allow for any real original work to occur.

Fresh Air and Natural Daylight.

A free-flowing circulation of fresh air and adequate natural daylight are essential to health, and when either are lacking there is impairment of concentration due to physical discomfort, associated headache, fatigue or irritability. Fresh air and natural daylight are needed for a free-flow of ideas and thoughts and are essential for innovation. An unhealthy environment constricts and narrows free expression because it is a stress, pressure and a distraction.

Pollution.

Pollution is a major factor in lowering vitality and the quality of life generally. Urban life is especially exposed to pollution factors which limit and undermine. Lead and exhaust fumes are the major factors but dust, smoke, hum, traffic and vibration noise all reduce concentration, inspiration, health and well-being.

Allergic Problems.

Creative thought is severely lessened by the generalised mucosal changes which characterise the allergic response. There is a thickening of mucosa in any area of the body with out-pouring of mucous and undermined general well-being and health. The sensitivity may be to milk, gluten, cheese, chocolate, shellfish, pollen, dust, animal-hair, feathers. Specific trees or plants – silver birch, rose, elder, daffodils, grasses – may also be the trigger, as house-mites in furniture and bedding. Underground streams, wells, water and ley-lines of energy sometimes provoke severe discomfort, not always easily diagnosed, with reactions of sneezing, congestion, sweating, hay-fever, asthma and cough. These chronic allergic mucosal reactions limit imaginative thinking as much as personal health and well-being.

Environmental Excesses and Exposure.

These include either lack of sun and warmth or excess exposure. Heat or cold can be a stress and an anti-creative factor. In a similar way lack of shelter or protection from wind and driving rain, with inadequate insulation, blinds or shade create atmospheric discomfort, distraction and undermines creative thinking because such stress factors limit and irritate psychologically as well as physically .

Chapter four

Social Blocks to Creativity

1. Pressures to Conform.

Every society imposes some limits, rules and pressures upon its members to adhere to established patterns, ideas, behaviour, dress and expression. These social limitations are closely allied to psychological ones and their development is fed by a combination of psychological, educational, media and religious factors. In general, such recommendations are more related to the interests of the establishment rather than those of individual expression, identity and personal growth. The aim of all social pressures is to control or limit rather than to support personal expansion and development. Social conformity aims at control of thought as well as self-expression and is as common in the large institution as within the family unit. Conformity is usually presented or packaged as a positive necessity or advantage, rather than a limitation of opportunity and expansion. This is clearly seen in the fashion world where commercial interest is presented as style and individuality. The advertising campaigns of the tobacco and liquor trade do the same thing advocating individuality or 'personality' with a product that suffocates it.

In a similar way an apparently open debate or political forum usually emphasises free-speech, communication and dialogue, when in fact it is doing the opposite. Both jargon and the media techniques keep truly open, questioning attitudes and perceptions minimal by a presentation which appears to have already done this for the individual by the interviewer. In this way marketing and interview techniques support conformity, control and passivity in society, limiting alternative thinking and questioning attitudes.

2. Lack of Opportunity for Questions.

Lack of opportunity for questions, clarification or dialogue is in itself a stress and a stimulation to fear and violence in some cases. The development of a new insight and new thinking is lessened by a climate which inhibits, because of inadequate opportunity for discussion. A tight budget, lack of time and other 'pressures' are usually blamed for the lack, but the end result is always a society where growth and the development of new ideas are severely cut back.

3. Lack of Information, Feedback and Dialogue.

An absence of feedback stimulation at any level limits innovative thought and leads to inhibition of response and ideas. Anti-social attitudes may be stimulated which may have a creative aspect to them but in general this is severely limited without the facilities of feedback and response.

4. Over-valuation of Authority Figures.

This may occur at either an institutional or individual level, with inappropriate excessive reactions and idealism based on denial. Over-valuing is always far removed from appreciation. Resentment quickly occurs because of the inequalities as well as idealisation. The 'expert' or consultant is felt to inhibit the individual because of feelings of inadequacy together with loss of discernment and judgement. When the pupil over-values the teacher, the patient his doctor, each loses by it because of unreal ideology and loss of personal esteem.

5. Passivity.

Closely related to over-valuation and the personality-cult of authoritarian figures, passivity is now one of the greatest problems that every healthy society has to deal with. Encouraged by the media, there is a tendency to accept easily what is given out as factual and relevant without question or comment. This often causes confusion and problems within the family as the overall passivity is seen by the adolescent as acceptance, or approval for behaviour patterns which the family find confusing or so radical that they fear responding.

6. Authoritarianism and the Abuse of Power.

This exists in the home or marriage, one partner dominating the other, or in a work-institution situation. In general the rule of 'closed shop' applies with imposed controls and restrictions, directly or indirectly to limit and control the other. The results are always a reduction of individual expression and output with minimal provision made for open debate, communication or disagreement.

7. Political Pressures.

These may be obviously imposed in an uncomfortable fashion, or more often subtle and indirect; the end result is the same however. Whatever form the pressure takes it is closely allied to authoritarian blocks and political pressures are just as unhealthy and undesirable as others where free expression of independent, thought is imposed upon. Controls and censorship aim only to impose values and patterns, to inhibit independent growth because it is 'difficult' challenging, uncomfortable or inconvenient.

8. Social Rigidity.

As in the other situations described the development of new, radical or different ways of thinking is discouraged or disallowed. It is common in our present exam-orientated educational system from the earliest age, with a single, correct or 'right' way of self-expression, rather than an individual one. An overall consideration of different possibilities of expression, rather than the single 'right' one, is highly desirable for creative growth. A broader approach is needed to encompass the individual viewpont as well as any formal approach to learning and problem-solving. Rigid, social structures like the media, family pressure, educational systems and religion tend to impose their ideas and standards as the only relevant ones, with minimal real concern or appreciation for the individual. Social conformity and rigidity leads to blockage, imposed patterns or moulds with personal realisation, individuality and creativity all inevitably lessened.

9. A Class Society.

A hierarchical system tends to reduce and limit the individual to a particular level or slot of expectation and conformity which has no relevance to individual aims and ability. The class system imposes its own rules, patterns, expectations and outlooks which limit personal realisation and growth. Originality is always seen as a threat to the system because it goes outside customary and established rules and limits at every level.

10. Opposition to Change.

The general attitude of others to personal change and growth has a direct relationship to creative expression and health. Too often there are pressures which impose known familiar patterns and attitudes to avoid challenge or change in a *status quo* of established behaviour and thinking. A woman with an obesity problem, but keeping to her diet, was told by a friend – "The first stone is not so difficult but you won't find it easy to lose any more". Also "You look haggard and drawn, it won't suit you to be thin". An agoraphobic woman was similarly told – "You may improve initially, but you must expect to slip back. You have done well so far, but the rest won't be so easy".

11. Education.

In many ways the most serious social block of all because it affects the young impressionable mind. With few exceptions, education is now only concerned with imposing an established fixed system of ideas and directions. Lip service is given to dialogue, pupil-discussion, and the development of alternative points of view at either teacher or pupil levels which could give a more meaningful, flexible approach to learning. The major concern of education is only success in the exam field and any deviation from required, set patterns of answers and syllabus is penalised and with it individuality. Education has become increasingly impersonal and as a result it is now at crisis point with both teachers and pupils disillusioned. In terms of personal development, new learning and creative expansion the results are disappointing. The advent of the language laboratory, television class and computer has led to even greater mechanical impersonal teaching, further removed from individual needs.

It is now almost impossible for either teacher, head, or pupil to be creative within the present system. New ideas or origination are uneconomic in terms of time, statistics and results and at any level are made difficult for financial reasons or discouraged because of the need for 'results' to avoid further penalties and cutbacks.

Put an average child in contact with another of the same age from a different culture and within a few days they will both be communicating and chattering away easily – probably in both languages. This would take years under our present system where practical results in the language class in terms of conversation and communication are appalling, often after years of study.

Old-fashioned ideas predominate within education and perpetuate rigid attitudes and a *status quo* causing limitation of confidence as well as real growth. Creative innovation has little place in a system where deviation from the set patterns is labelled as 'bad' when not definitely discouraged. As classes merge and get larger, under pressure, with problems of discipline and re-organisation, the bright child becomes increasingly bored, indifferent and difficult and the integrated one more deprived or isolated. Both suffer from the lack of creative attention and the individual approach which is needed.

The few exceptions that occur in the educational field are in schools with small classes where some individual attention is still maintained in spite of the pressures. Usually there is a highly individual teacher, exceptional in interests and having escaped being dragged down by a repressive establishment. In some fields, especially art and design, the standards of creative originality are at times outstanding – which confirms my viewpoint that it is the system which is at fault rather than any absence of creativity in the child.

12. Religion.

When religion is only concerned with dogma, absolutes, convictions and certainties, it has lost its simplicity and is as limiting as the present education system. Doubts and uncertainties should be at the heart of every healthy growing religion, a matter of dialogue, discussion and concern, rather than one of failure, guilt or inadequacy. Loss of faith and belief happens at some time to everyone and needs to be sensitively assessed, not a matter for self-reproach or punishment. Where there is a more imaginative approach to personal problems of faith and beliefs which are at variance with dogma, then a more healthy attitude prevails. When uncertainty, doubt and not-knowing are acceptable there is opportunity to explore them. This is always positive for the individual. Religion is a powerful establishment for fostering superstition, and where faith has been lost, there is also loss of confidence and hope. An overall viewpoint which can tolerate uncertainty and not-knowing is essential to a healthy religion and a balanced creative individual.

13. Upbringing.

Upbringing is the most important of all social blocks. Society imposes blocks on attitudes towards divorce, abortion, conception, pregnancy, childbirth, contraception and breast-feeding, as well as child-caring and parental-closeness. Some aspects of creativity already begin with attitudes towards conception and pregnancy. A natural warm spontaneous feeling in the mother of being valued and accepted is communicated to the growing foetus and makes for security and spontaneity of self-expression. The attitude of both parents and the family as a whole are important during the pregnancy as much as the mother's psychological and environmental health.

Infection, diet, noise, the social-addictive habits, especially smoking, limit the growth of the growing foetus and reflect the overall health and vitality of the mother. A birth, well-prepared for by midwife, doctor and obstetrician, physically as well as psychologically, keeps anxiety and stress to a minimum. Where there is anguish, disapproval, lack of preparation and inadequate caring, these make for a more difficult birth, an anxious mother and baby. When social attitudes to birth are open with the father present then the chances of a normal confinement and a healthy child are optimised. Society imposes rules and value-judgements on breast-feeding, rest and handling a child which can undermine or deviate parents away from their needs and natural instincts. Attitudes towards holding, feeding and bed-time are too often socially imposed rather than reflecting the family, culture and mother-child relationship. Where values are flexible, rather than ritualistic, relating to the needs and temperament of the individual, then growth, creativity and individuality are optimum. When rules and behaviour-control are meaningful, and punishment a part of the expression of a caring sensitive family, it is not limiting or damaging and makes for a more healthy creative child. Fixed ideas, conformity, patterns and custom with no reference to the individual at the time stifle creativity because they reflect attitudes of a system rather than those of the person.

Chapter five

Overcoming Social Blocks to Creativity

1.Stimulate Awareness, Openness and Honesty.

Use discussion, debate and a more spontaneous expression of feelings and ideas. In every educational situation, dialogue is needed between both teachers and teachers and pupils. Discussion should be encouraged at each level with opportunity to discuss doubts and criticism and to raise problems such as cuts, limitations and reasons without this being a threat in any way.

2. Change the Environment Externally.

Consider a move to another school, job, town, university or country. Also consider a totally new field of expression, work or endeavour, however specialised or committed you are.

There is always a time and a reason for change as long as it is not a repetitive flight pattern but one of creative expression and growth.

3. Change the Environment Internally.

Consider changing thought patterns, assumptions and attitudes by more active protest. Marching, meetings, pressure-groups, writing and using the media may all help to express a viewpoint. Avoid violence but public speech should be available in a healthy society. If this is not the case you may have to use indirect, less public channels. Always be sure, as you protest and aim to change attitudes, that you are not being rigid, autocratic and repressive yourself.

4. Avoid Ritual and Dogma.

When forming or joining a group of similar-minded people, avoid ritual, patterns and rigid dogmatic assumptions. Be as creative and questioning in the group as towards those you are trying to change and influence. Avoid judgement and certainty by being open-minded, listening and fair at all times.

5. Consider Alternatives.

Express creative ideas and intentions directly whenever possible but where these are blocked for any reason, consider indirect alternatives. For example if you want to work with deprived children or those with special needs but your superior refuses to support you, then work voluntarily at weekends and holidays, perhaps abroad as a helper. Join voluntary organisations. Try to help, develop, research and write up your experiences. Talk about them in the week with friends and colleagues.

6.Change Directions.

Consider totally changing your directions and aims to others that are more realistic and available in new areas, even a different country or environment which you feel is more supportive and progressive. Don't fear or avoid making a change when it seems positive with potential for growth.

7. Look at your own Motivations.

Analyse closely your own attitudes and expectations to ensure that the faults and blockages are not within yourself and projected into the environment. Be sure that you are delegating enough, sharing and not being intolerant, giving and contributing new ideas, energy, supportive of others and *their* initiatives, levels of growth and development.

8.Vary Working Patterns.

Where the environment has no privacy or quiet area for work and thought, consider working different hours, flexi-time, so that early mornings or late evenings give time for quiet thinking. Alter working habits and patterns to improve problems in the environment. If you cannot alter or move within the environment, then change yourself to be less affected or irritated by it. Try to be less patterned and rigid, less susceptible to outside pressures and happenings, less blown by the winds of change, events and circumstances.

9.Become less Dependent.

In general be more independent and less dependent on the environment and its trappings. Be more self-supportive whenever possible, less affected or influenced by others. Outside externals should affect you less, be less undermining and less of an intrusion. Always remember that externals are only as much of an intrusion as you yourself allow them to be.

Chapter six

Cultural Blocks to Creativity

Cultural pressures and blocks are on the whole more subtle than social or environmental ones because they are less obvious, usually labelled as 'good' or desirable from infancy onwards. Such pressures tend however to impose and dictate a value system upon others which undermines rather than develops individuality and creativity. Cultural blocks impose a morality as to what is right or wrong, a direction of behaviour which take no account of individuality. These pressures are not easily confronted or reasoned with because they seem natural and an unquestionable part of our heritage. Yet they can be the most harmful factors in blocking of personal growth and development because new thinking and other approaches are undermined and limited by what is 'best and traditional' for the individual.

Superstition.

These are primitive magical beliefs present in every society which act as powerful limiting factors to control change and individual action. They are always fed by isolation, lack of feedback and ignorance, also by fear and partial information. In general their aim is to preserve the *status quo* and to keep information at an infantile, phantasy-dominated level, rather than healthy, questioning and explorative.

'Tradition'.

Tradition is less about cultural values and more about the ways that families and societies control its members and direct others. It is usually a mixture of superstition, dogma and ideology which may at times maintain a useful balance between too rapid growth and links with the past. It is usually dominated by old-fashioned customs and language which have little practical relevance to an evolving present.

Chapter seven

Psychological Blocks to Creativity

1. Overwhelming Emotional Reactions.

Excessive anxiety, fear, over-reaction of any kind to the new tend to block and control. The anticipation of failure that a challenge cannot be met or overcome adds to difficulty, especially when waiting the outcome of a problem. Control is expressed by repetition of familiar patterns and attitudes, re-enacted in a wide variety of different situations.

2. Negative Certainty.

Paralyses and limits by its very certainty and lack of questioning. There is a repetition of failure imagery which constantly reinforces anxieties and uncertainties, to paralyse all creative imaginative development and also experimentation and change.

3. Self-Doubt.

Where there is lack of confidence and self-doubt there is also inhibition and withdrawal so that limits and tight boundaries are set to every situation reducing the development of ideas and perceptions. Everything tends to be interpreted in terms of failure or failure-possibility which limits growth and the expansion of ideas, in case they do not come up to a phantasised ideal.

4. Negative Criticism.

Destructive criticism blocks and then reinforces fears and uncertainties creating negative emotion which undermines confidence and play. Experimenting with new situations, relationships, ideas and structures is kept minimal in case there is loss of face, hurt pride or bruised vanity. Confidence becomes totally worn-down so that drive and effort are paralysed.

Only an outburst of rage or resentment may at times provoke a more positive response, a different viewpoint because of loss of control. Often however the outcome is failure of creative drive rather than any increase in determination and creative endeavour.

5. Lack of Support and Encouragement.

The absence of positive backing and support creates a negative psychological climate, also an unhealthy dependence so that anxiety builds up and confidence is lost. The formation of a negative focus blocks freedom of thought, association and the development of new ideas.

6. Impatience and the Inability to Delay.

Here the individual attempts to impose familiar, usually negative patterns and formulations upon each new situation, because there is intolerance of the time required to understand and relate to an expanding new. Cliché-understanding seems preferable to making the necessary internal changes and adjustments to encompass new situations and the challenge they pose. Pressure and intolerance, demands for immediate solutions and knowing are typical symptoms.

7. Lack of Imaginative Ideas or Solutions.

The inability to see new ideas or solutions in a challenging and potential growth situation is because innovation and imaginative expression are blocked by assumption of difficulty, impossibility or failure. The usual underlying cause is that change to the *status quo*, even of new awareness and growth, is a threat to security.

8. Rigidity and Control.

In general, known familiar patterns of response are preferred because they are more comfortable. Familiar ideas and thought-patterns of response are used to limit spontaneity and break-through of illumination and insight. These boundaries of fixed assumption and pattern control unconscious fears of failure and rejection.

9. Excessive Conformity.

Attitudes of placating, appeasing, reassuring others are based on fear and concern for psychological safety, maintaining the *status quo* of attitudes, ideas, developing perception and awareness. The aim is to form a web of self-limiting conformity and knowing under the mistaken belief that it maintains security, acceptance and approval.

10. Routine Attitudes.

These are common and based on fixed ideas, habits and attitudes which mislead, are unimaginative or repetitive. They relate to a need to control spontaneity, movement of ideas, to create patterns of predictable habit, limiting changes of perspective and new associations. In this way new directions of insight and understanding tend to be blocked by routine.

11. Boredom and Lack of Interest.

The common psychological reasons for states of boredom are depression, grief, shock or emotional trauma. These paralyse emotional sensitivity and response in a futile attempt to freeze feeling, awareness and self to avoid either pain or vulnerability. The lack of interest and stimulation intensifies depression, rather than resolving it, and the absence of involvement, energy and drive is an additional cause for anxiety so that the original problem becomes a pressure situation.

12. Lack of Confidence.

A constant negative viewpoint of doubt, fear or failure with inability to respond to a particular challenge or demand leads to feelings of inadequancy, anxiety and a tendency to withdraw. Contact with others is sometimes completely undermined or lost as initiative and identity are weakened.

13. A Personal Emotional Crisis.

Excessive, intense feelings and over-reaction lead to paralysed creative initiative. Judgement, feelings, identity, innovation and creative response are lost or 'washed over' by a tide of emotion and feelings, affecting balance and an imaginative viewpoint.

14. Prejudice.

A harsh, judgemental, rigid, viewpoint limits fresh thinking, change of position and understanding so that insights and new perception cannot develop and with them growth. It is related to a particularly hard, censuring conscience, strict disciplinarian attitudes, negating and self-critical attitudes which are ultimately destructive.

15. Preserving the Status Quo.

Opposition to change and innovation stems from fear or the conviction of disaster. In this way it imposes known, repetitive attitudes of thinking and view-points over response and spontaneity. A brake is applied to each emerging situation as differing responses are carefully controlled or limited, and with them growth and development. The boundaries of thought, understanding and awareness are kept narrow, to familiar, well-defined areas, the emphasis on limits, caution, suspicion and control, rather than experience, change and spontaneity.

16. Over-Emphasis on Externals as a Flight from Sensitive Awareness.

Where the emphasis is on externals as the only tangible reality, the concrete, label and cliché or recipe, this keeps all life experience to superficial, contrived levels of reality. Here the pose and the personality are more important and emphasised than real depths of a situation and ultimate alternatives for growth, development and change. Weakness is inevitably the outcome of such externals and with it a sense of vulnerability which paralyses new initiative and innovation. As more intangible, internal aspects of a situation are denied or repressed, so too is intangible, explorative thought, new links, awareness and personal growth.

17. Insecurity.

An environment where there is undue fear, danger or violence arouses protective anxiety and lessens more creative thought. Primary security and survival takes priority over new-development, unless in the service of safety when creative thinking can be to the fore. The wooden escape horse of the P.O.W. camp was an example of ingenuity and the most original creative plans have often been evoked in the service of escape and survival. But in general threats of eviction, take-over, redundancy, premature retirement or delayed promotion act as barriers to development rather than as a stimulus to change, imagination and growth.

18. Excessive Psychological Environmental Pressures.

These include personal dislike or hates, excessive rivalry, jealousy, constant destructive negative criticism, fears and doubt which undermines confidence or overwhelms the creative processes. A negative environment creates a negative internal state which is ultimately destructive, and paralysing to creative thinking. Where an excess of feelings takes over innovation, this usually reflects underlying insecurity or anxiety.

19. Institutionalisation.

Living or working in a community, or large unit which is too impersonal to provide individual care and attention, perhaps a large school, dormitory, hospital ward or factory, tends to encourage regression and a return to infantile patterns and needs. This re-emergence of earlier fears and attitudes is a barrier to creativity because adult as well as infantile aspects of the self must be freely available and flexible with neither in a dominant position over the other.

20. An Impersonal Work Environment.

Usually such situations are far too large and remote for the individual to contain and relate to. There is a sense of being 'lost in a crowd' or loss of personal identity is threatened. It is common in a large, open-plan office where innovation and change are minimal if they occur at all. Sometimes there are deliberate attempts to undermine, divert or mislead. In a competitive situation, concentration and attention may be deliberately undermined to block others from thinking or gaining an advantage.

21. Political Intrusion.

This includes pressures to protest, strike, or conform to propaganda, which is at variance with the intentions and wishes of the individual. Where pressures are considerable, individuality is lost and with it independent personal creativity. Development and growth are diverted by 'known' conclusions, rigid standards, beliefs and convictions which exclude the expression of individual ideas and personal feelings.

22. Passivity.

There is undue acceptance of the authority of others including their conclusions and often directions. A significant lack of criticism, independent view-point and challenge occurs as personality and drive are taken over. This may be further combined with unhealthy idealisation of authoritarian figures. In general a passive environment encourages 'blind' obedience and discourages independent thought, individuality or questioning. It is common in the large institution, union, or church with emphasis on rules, policy and doctrine rather than the needs and realities of individual members. Lack of questioning or disagreement lead to blocked thought areas which cannot be questioned because they are 'holy cows', matters of dogma and authority which cannot be challenged. In many families during childhood and frequently in later years sex, religion and politics are taboo subjects at meal times, even prohibited at other times. In this way they become areas of fixation and frustration, their growth and integration isolated and eventually a block to development and growth.

23. The Fear of Making Mistakes and Looking Foolish.

Because of an excessive emphasis on being correct, rewarded as 'right', good and worthy of praise, fear develops at the same time of being 'wrong', unloved, rejected and foolish. Fear is of not knowing and admitting it. Emphasis on the fixed, absolute right makes for insecurity and is largely the result of faulty upbringing attitudes, with over-emphasis on success and achievement, rather than personal development. Making a mistake, becomes an embarrassment, leading to loss of confidence, shame or humiliation. Emphasis is on correctness and order rather than to explore and use every experience as a platform to test and experience new assumptions, new thinking and extending the self. Changing boundaries, points of reference and assumption are essential to all innovation and learning. The man who never makes a mistake is a liar or a fool. In general it is a mistake to over-emphasise being either right or wrong, as long as each experience leads to further knowledge, experimentation and learning.

Chapter eight

Overcoming Environmental Blocks to Creativity

I. Compensate for unsatisfactory urban life by taking time off in the country whenever possible. Get out of doors in an area where you can safely be quiet and walk away from pressures and in contact with nature. In this way internal blocks and external pressures can be reduced, put more into perspective. Where rural isolation is the problem, loneliness a stress, change frequently to more stimulating, non-stressful environments when necessary, but use the quiet of the country to develop and elaborate strength, energy and ideas as they occur.

2. As much as possible, open doors and windows so that fresh air and natural daylight can stimulate a flow of vitality, well-being and ideas. Changes of climate, environment and work can be a stimulation to new ideas

developing, becoming more open and available to look, learn and see how others approach a particular problem in their own unique and individual creative way.

3. Visualise a pleasant quiet environment, when relaxing, ideally one which you know well, and use the principles of positive imagery and confident expectation. This is particularly useful when under pressure, waiting for an idea to develop or expand or for a new solutions to become apparent.

4. Find a particular space or area that suits you where you can relax psychologically as well as physically, able to be yourself. It may be either inside, or outside, in the country, library or park. But find somewhere comfortable where you can think, feel and be unpressurised. Find also the right time of day, when you feel at optimum, in this way combining your space with the best timing. You may also find that there is a particular season of the year when you are more 'centred' and actively creative.

5. Take regular exercise as well as sleep and don't be pressurised or overwhelmed by a particular problem. If this happens the problem is running you and not you the problem. See

every problem, every worry as a challenge only and an unresolved, undeclared solution. Don't sit at home worrying and not sleeping. If this tends to happen be much more positive in your attitude to the worry. Do what you can do *now* to the full and spend some time talking with a sympathetic friend. Always take a definite positive action which is relevant and await the outcome. In this way you minimise stress.

6. Avoid all social addictives as much as possible, especially tea, coffee, smoking and alcohol. Take them if required by the social situation, but not regularly, and in moderation. They are habit-forming and reinforce fixed patterns which are opposed to creativity. Also take synthetic pharmaceutical drugs to a minimum, only when absolutely necessary, and always closely question your doctor as to their necessity as well as the dangers. If you feel that there is over-prescribing of synthetic drugs, don't hesitate to get another opinion. Most drugs sedate and lead to dependency, with loss of energy and drive after a brief period of symptom-relief or stimulation. The addictive drugs such as marihuana, cocaine or heroin have the myth of being stimulating, but it is only a myth and their addictive properties narrow and intensify barriers and boundaries rather than broadening true creative aware-ness, growth and confidence.

7. Consider forming a small discussion group of three-four people, in this way creating a limited environment of trust and openness where you can talk and share new, developing ideas without negative criticism. In this way negative inhibition and judgement can be kept minimal and it may be possible to develop new ways of discussing and exchanging unpolished ideas to form new links and associations. But every group, once formed, must also grow, evolve, change, and develop, like anything else in nature and you must not expect to stay static or that it will always be the same. With like-minded people, you can bounce-off ideas, thoughts and phantasies, loosen-up more imaginative concepts in an original non-critical, fun way, so that it is neither deadly serious or too intense with humour and balance lost. In general this can only happen in small groups and is one of their major advantages.

8. Whenever the environment feels critical, hostile or non-supportive, find a close circle of friends who you can talk with and relate to. Where the work environment is rigid, unsympathetic and non-supportive to innovation, keep both emotional and creative resources more to yourself. When you are dependent on a particular job for income and cannot make a change, then withdraw emotional involvement from the front-line and quietly do your work but not more than is required. Where the hostile

environment is at home, within the family, then indirect expressions of your creative self may avoid an immediate acute conflict situation until either there is a change within yourself or you are able and strong enough to make a move and be more separate.

9   In general read, listen, talk and travel. Communicate at different levels with as many people as possible, especially in your field of special interest, activity and knowledge.

10. Be self-reliant, giving to others yet not totally dependent upon them. Realise that it is your own attitudes and example that change others.

11. Gain further insight and understanding by observation and contact with nature – the persistence of a spider, bee or ant. Discover new insights into 'difficult' situations by seeing how other, simpler forms of life overcome blocks and hurdles. The simple can be just as rewarding as the scientific and literary. The simplicity of a flower can be a stimulus to greater calm and an incentive to new perceptions and insights. Try to be less dependent upon formal, environ-mental externals, establishment-thinking and attitudes, much of which are ritualistic and

traditional. Look more for confirmation of ideas and new approaches, by getting outside routine and closer to the energy of nature.

Chapter nine

Environmental Factors that Encourage Creativity

1. Congenial surrounds, a well-proportioned room, daylight with circulation of fresh-air, a comfortable temperature with pleasing tones and decor, all help relaxation, balance and harmony. A well-proportioned building with the best of modern planning and architecture gives priority to space, lay-out and surroundings, aware of the importance of landscaping, light and insulation. In a similar way, convenience of access is important to shops, schools and transport. Where all of these factors have been taken into account, the surroundings and accommodation give maximum support to original ideas and creativity because the environment does not impose, irritate or limit in any way. A badly planned home or office is a stress and a pressure causing the build-up of physical and psychological factors which block creativity. Over-crowding, stale air, cigarette

smoke, traffic fumes, noise are distractions. Where there is dependency upon background noise, an environment that is too quiet may be upsetting, even intolerable. In general the facilities of a regular, quiet room with a minimum of interference is ideal, but always depending upon individual temperament.

Other distractions are the telephone, demands of friends, neighbours or colleagues. The ideal is a personal room where for some part of the day you can be quiet and 'unavailable', undisturbed with immediate access controlled or delayed. A secretary is ideal but not always possible, and a closed door or note – 'unavailable at present', may be adequate against most intrusions.

2. A flexible supportive encouraging environment, tolerant of new or unformed ideas and incomplete thinking is important. Support with lack of opposition to change or innovation is ideal. An environment where immediate criticism of suggestions and ideas is minimal with dialogue possible without immediate negatives gives maximum stimulus to new insights and thought-awareness.

3. A flexible, non-autocratic work or home situation with a parent, teacher or colleague who is open-minded, prepared to show interest and give support without immediate opposition

yet prepared to criticise or comment. Freedom from excessive psychological and physical pressures with a superior able to delegate, share and be supportive of new suggestions and ideas.

4. The ability and facility to refer back to past experience with access to current information is usually essential for growth and innovation. This may be a library or computer, depending upon individual needs and the stage of development of a creative idea. A modern information service is not always essential to creative thought in the early stages, but is likely to be needed at some time during the processes of elaboration and development.

5. Security with a sense of personal safety is basic, supporting ease and relaxation with psychological pressures, threats and fears minimal. An environment which gives a secure future for a reasonable period facilitates planning to take place. Closures, threats of redundancy, having to change, move, look for another house, job or school are stresses and distractions which undermine and drain the level of creativity.

A General Summary of how best to Overcome Environmental Blocks to Creativity.

1. Eat and live healthily, avoiding fast ideas or fast food which undermine body and mind of originality and vitality.

2. Develop regular habits for eating and sleeping. Eat slowly, with a balanced diet to counter-balance a stressful lifestyle and to maximise health.

3. Develop regular periods of quiet, relaxation and stillness.

4. If your life is centred mainly in the city, have regular quite periods in the country, in contact with nature.

5. Travel as much as possible, with contacts, discussion and wider reading in new areas of interest and stimulus.

6. If the environment cannot be changed, then relax and go with it more, accepting it for as long as is necessary, rather than always fighting it and complaining.

7. Create new alternative stimulating areas with new people, new ideas and new contacts.

8. Change the more static areas of your life by innovation and suggestion, especially overcoming possessiveness, jealousy, and control by more healthy psychological attitudes.

9. Understand the needs of others more, including those who share your environment.

10. Optimise health by living and working in an environment where atmospheric pollution is minimal or at least at acceptable levels.

11. Change yourself if you cannot change others; in this way you will indirectly influence them and reduce the build-up of anti-creative resentment and stress-negatives.

12. Consider changing aims as well as attitudes. Re-consider regularly your directions and priorities and be sure that these still reflect you as you are *now* and have not become rigid inflexible patterns.

13. Change your environment also by lobbying your M.P., discussion and publicity. Set an example that will in itself inspire and bring about change. Become knowledgeable and an expert in your own field so that you are needed if not indispensable. Give more to soften hard attitudes in others and to lessen rigidity.

Chapter ten

Psychological Factors that Encourage Creativity

1. Interest and Motivation.

When interest is combined with a sense of pleasure, interest or fulfilment the involvement gives a satisfaction that supports drive and energies to explore and develop. Experimentation, experiencing some frustration or limitation,with the need to develop alternatives combine together as new thinking and creativity.

2. Personal Dissatisfaction and Frustration with the Present.

A combination of concern with some urgency for change, to get something finished, stimulates new ways of looking and thinking. The ability and willingness to accept some frustration, but not to abandon, combined with insistence or persistence for a different solution leads to new outcomes. Refusal to accept the conventional, the fashionable and the limited leads also to determination to change and to new ways or solutions.

3. Confident Visualisation of the End-Result as both Positive and Inevitable.

Where there is a steady thought-image of success and achievement, the intermediate steps for making it a tangible reality occur unconsciously, as long as there is no extreme pressure or a time-schedule for the changes to take place.

4. Patience without Pressure.

The ability to tolerate waiting for a solution without imposing self-pressures is basic to creativity. In this way, with confidence in the outcome, new ideas 'incubate', evolve and have enough time to develop and link-up with previous experience and knowledge. Pressure is always destructive and the quick, hurried solution is uncreative, solely for reassurance, to avoid uncertainty before new insights and perspectives become more obvious.

5. The Ability to Tolerate some Chaos, Mess and Confusion.

Closely allied to the need for patience is willingness to accept an apparently messy, partial, unknown situation or hypothesis as the only possible position at that time before a further link or clarification is made. Some intrinsic chaos is inseparable from every creative procedure and when it cannot be tolerated for reasons of insecurity then the developmental cycle may be broken. During this period, the unconscious is at work, making links and scanning possible, new relationships and ties within a more fluid, broken-down situation to give maximum and new approximation of previously unlinked areas.

6. Relaxation and Freedom from Overwhelming Anxiety.

Freedom from overwhelming, intrusive anxiety is essential for creative work to take place because it distracts and absorbs energy needed for wider association-work. Being relaxed, the unconscious is given maximum freedom of origination so that a truly individual response is possible once fear and self-interest are minimal.

7. Being Well-briefed.

Well-briefed, background information, like wide experience, is basic to every creative experience in order to bring the most divergent, different, contrasting experiences into focus and relationship. Where this occurs, in as many different, divergent ways without prejudgement, new arrangements of concepts can occur and initiate the creative process.

8. Support and Encouragement from Others.

A supportive, encouraging, positive psychological environment gives added strength to conscious endeavours to be daring and breakaway from patterns and partial solutions.

9. The Ability to Play and Juggle with Seemingly Unrelated Ideas.

Play is essential to creative health as much as humour and is often related. Whenever unrelated ideas can be juggled and moved around, re-positioned, or put into unlikely or 'impossible' positions, breaking the rules, this may lead to new insights. A creative position is commonly the juxta-positioning of unlikely thoughts and ideas. Surprise is basic to both comedy and creativity.

10. A Non-judgemental Attitude and Freedom from Negative Criticism.

Most people have a tendency to be negative about themselves in some way or other and to be self-destructive in opinions and judgements whatever the realities. When such masochistic negatives are kept minimal this helps preserve the fragile, early stages of creative linkage and growth .

11. The Ability to Let Go of a Problem.

Standing back from the immediacy of a problem or conclusion supports wider perspectives and judgement because immediacy is given less impact. In this way the links which develop are more independent of unconscious controlling associations and prejudgements, with less interference in developing associations.

12. More open Attitudes to Unfamiliar, 'Inconvenient' Facts and Ideas.

An open mind with the honesty to accept and not deny new or 'difficult' facts not obviously fitting the etablished picture, is a major factor for innovation, new trains of thought and association. The refusal to deny inconvenient 'exceptional' material is creative integrity and supports new patterns and ideas. Tolerance of links and associations not obviously relevant at the time is often a key stage in the emergence of new recognition and new associations.

13. A Healthy Psychological Environment.

Where there is tolerance and respect for new ideas and 'alternative' suggestions, they can usually be listened to, discussed and responded to if not seen as a threat. When discussion is based on trust, sharing and spontaneity of feeling, then immediacy of response and association is encouraged and fear, controls, mistrust and rigidity are kept minimal.

Chapter eleven

Overcoming Blocks to Creativity

1. Adapt Attitudes of Confident Expectation and Certainty.

Think, visualise, positively and confidently. Expect a positive outcome. Do not allow fear or doubt to come into your mind.

2. Clearly Visualise the Positive Outcome.

Hold the desired end-result as an image clearly in your mind and do this daily without concern for the intermediate steps. Never accept a first or immediate partial solution as necessarily the best and be prepared for a later, delayed one to emerge.

3. Take Non-Judgemental Attitudes.

In order to foster a positive, creative psychological environment that can link seemingly unrelated events, it is important that this internal milieu is in balance. A non-judgemental, non-comment, observing approach to a problem or challenge is best, allowing new associations and ideas to develop. It should be possible to tolerate mistakes or failures and to accept them as inevitable stepping-stones in the development of new awareness and insight.

4. Take a More Confident Relaxed Approach.

Be as relaxed as possible in your approach to a challenge to give yourself maximum time when problem-solving. Minimise anxiety and tension by being relaxed to support the emergence of new perceptions, insights and relationships.

5. Practise Exercises that Develop Imagination.

Use any of the specific exercises recommended which seem relevant to your particular block or need. It is important too however to develop your own exercises, especially in areas where you are most inhibited or where the recommended exercises are either insufficient or imprecise for your particular need and blockage.

6. Overcome Failure-Concepts and Fears.

Be quite definite about negative thought patterns. They are totally opposed to original growth and unconsciously designed to prevent change and new thinking. Refuse to allow fears and negatives to dominate or paralyse your thinking and free-flow of ideas. Negative failure-thinking is always aimed at blocking change and seeks to impose its own patterns of pessimism to colour and inhibit.

7. Look back at Previous Areas of Past Problem-Solving Experience for greater Perspective.

From time to time, look back and learn from past situations which previously you thought were irresolvable. Remind yourself of how you thought and acted then at that time and how they were eventually resolved. Ask yourself if new creative ideas, expressions and changes were an outcome of that difficulty and challenge. Did your mood of the time intensify a psychological blockage or were your attitudes a stimulus and support to new thinking and solutions emerging.

8. Take the Pressure off Yourself whenever Possible.

Free yourself mentally from anxiety as well as from tangible external preoccupations which distract, control or limit you. Give yourself maximum opportunity for creative thinking to take place without the weight of restriction, judgement or time-table. Try to be more of an ally to your creative thought rather than an obstruction and an enemy to it.

9. Be more Willing to Take a Chance.

Be much more prepared to expose yourself to new ideas, people and experience without feeling vulnerable. Experimentation and new contacts are part of life and basic to learning and any new approach. Try to be more open, daring and different with each new situation. Have the courage to do something different without fearing failure or being wrong. Be prepared to attempt spontaneous, alternative approaches to everyday situations. In general be different and try to get outside usual routine without fear or anxiety. If something goes wrong, is different or unexpected, accept this as part of outcome and learning from the exercise. All too often wrong means different and an experience outside the expected is one less controlled. Often too an apparent setback is just the beginning of a new pathway and a new you.

Chapter twelve

Attitudes that Develop Creative Potential

1. Independence.

A certain degree of independence is desirable, indeed essential for creative thinking. The imposed pressures and viewpoints of others sets limits and restrictions, especially those of conformity which are unhealthy and counter-productive. An inter-dependent attitude of mutual respect for the viewpoints attitudes and individuality of others is much more positively supportive to change and growth.

2. Opposition to Interruption and Distraction.

A firm approach to outside distraction is essential to free and maintain a consistent thread of thoughts and ideas without deviation so that the unconscious processes of trial and error, experiment, comparing and approximation can occur during the incubation or developmental phase of creativity.

3. Giving Attention to Essentials.

The creative mind is a flexible sensitive one. You should be aware of peripheral ideas but not be dominated, deviated or displaced by them, unless you want to be, and they provide a thread or link-line to what is being developed. More important is allowing unusual associations to seemingly unrelated concepts and ideas to come up for evaluation and possible link-association.

4. Listen More Attentively.

When listening, try to keep personal preoccupations out so that it is not a narcissistic repetitive theme, displacing new thinking and ideas as these emerge. Keep personal phantasies out of dialogue and in general listen more attentively so that there is a central, integral flow of new ideas, responses and sharing, rather than a repetitive tangential distraction as a barrier to change and contact.

5. Give Attention to Underlying Principles being Developed.

Where there is a definite goal, direction and theme these should be explored and thoroughly understood so that you are quite familiar with the basic principles underlying each new development. This gives depth and meaning to new relationships and expressions of creativeness providing a framework to develop and extend it.

6. Access to Data and Background Information.

Whatever the task in hand, access to facts and data are required at some time, whether the creative field is artistic or scientific. Background information is essential because it allows experience and comparision of existing ideas with past thought. In general background data is less valuable for the initial development of ideas but comes more into place during the later processes of expansion, practical development and application.

7. Supporting Others Who Are Also Working with New Approaches and Ideas.

Always give maximum time and support to others working in the field of creative original ideas. In this way you help stimulate them as well as helping in the development of a pool of origination which ultimately supports your own innovation and sensitivity.

8. Develop Overall Understanding rather than a Specialised One.

Try to avoid concentrating only on one particular area of interest or concept to the exclusion of others. This is limiting and unimaginative. Take a more total, overall direction with each new thought and idea as it emerges, allowing details to be filled in later. Once a theme is established and recognised, former ways of thinking and perceiving can be gradually relinquished.

Chapter thirteen

Exercises to Overcome Psychological Blocks to Creativity

1. Practise delay in coming to conclusions, suspending judgement in everyday events and happenings. Delay too, emotional reactions to frustrations which would normally overwhelm you. Practise a more relaxed, 'hung back', uncertain approach to daily situations. Especially avoid immediacy, conviction and precipitant responses to events with rapid conclusions. Such attitudes invariably defeat every original approach, however spontaneous they may seem. They usually reflect insecurity, 'short-fuse', patterns of control and assertion to reinforce pre-judgement and premature conclusions rather than a developing, evolving, growing new.

2. Stay calm and relaxed in annoying frustrating moments as they happen. At such times, practise being cool. Calmness under

pressure and stress is more valuable than at other times. You should not be controlled at such times, but physically relaxed and psychologically in balance, aware yet calm. The true significance of annoyance and its relevance to growth and creative development should also be understood. Avoid violent swings of emotion at all times and responses that overwhelm, to give an emotional landslide. Practise regularly and daily, but particularly at times of stress and challenge.

3. Phantasise a situation where someone important to you is being rejecting or hurtful. Instead of feeling hurt or angry, find a reason to understand and explain the reasons behind their attitude. In this way make sense of their behaviour so that it is tolerable and acceptable. Feel yourself relaxing. See yourself as calm and not carried away by the feelings of the situation. Now repair the hurt or rebuff and explain and experience your feelings and reasons to the other.

4. Visualise a flower of your own choosing. Take it back to earliest origins – a seed, cutting, or graft through the seasons of the year. See it root, grow and evolve. Let it clearly change and mature through its different cycles and stages of growth as well as of rest. Now feel yourself change, evolve and grow too as you pass through your own stages of surge, growth, quiet and pause. Feel your affinity with the flower and try to visualise its colours as they emerge and its distinctive perfume.

5. Visualise a known familiar situation, which is definite and certain to you without question. For example that $2+2=4$. Now prove that it is a fallacy and only relatively true. Find alternative answers to familiar, known certainties testing your basic assumptions about facts beyond dispute and question. You will find that they exist in a wide variety of areas and lead to rigid controls, boundaries and assumptions which limit growth and awareness. Test basic assumption areas, as the sky is blue, trees green and demonstrate the alternative answers – for example in cataract or colour-blindness. If necessary research the question in your local library. Extend your own examples and develop new thinking and ideas in these areas. The aim is to break down rigid assumption in every area, even the most common place. 'Factual', assumption-thinking with pre-formed conclusions defeats creativity before it can be elaborated.

For example, the assumption that $2+2=4$ is a fallacy because it is too absolute. There are no absolutes in anything, the whole of life is changing, evolving, expanding, contracting, aging and maturing in some way. An expanding, changing, evolving 2 of anything + another equally evolving changing duality, gives a 4 in movement which is + or – and in a state of flux and change at any given moment.

Paint or draw a familiar subject in your environment – a tree, garden-seat or your street. Paint it first as you think of it – solid with quite definite colours, a transparent familiar background of blue sky and green grass. Now reverse it all, painting the tree or chosen object in the negative and transparent with the surroundings solid. Experiment further by changing colours. Paint the tree-trunk blue, the sky brown, road green, grass grey or mauve. In this way you will be trying to break-down familiar situations that reduce new perceptions by assumption or imposing rigid boundaries which limit. These are too rigidly defined with too much certainty and insufficient awareness of what is actually present and happening. Once the exercises are developed and elaborated, you can create with them, as outlines, shapes and boundaries become less rigid, less confining and limiting. Aim to see the familiar in a new fresh, original way, rather than as something fixed or taken for granted so that it is not really seen at all. The fixed image inside you makes looking superfluous, and reality-appraisal no longer necessary. In this way we look as if blind, without seeing, because we KNOW what things are and don't need to see any more. Try to lessen these visual as-sumption-patterns to familiar everyday situations. Discover them, then break through their fixed barriers. Find other areas where you are equally closed up, blind and certain.

Chapter fourteen

Exercises to Expand Creativity

1. Stimulate a broader, more overall awareness of each daily experience. Try to visualise everyday things in as many different ways as possible. Realise the component parts of every experience. For example when posting a letter, try to separate-out walking from posting and the box itself. As part of this exercise visualise quite separate areas for each stage of walking, writing a letter, making a cake, mowing the lawn. Juggle the components, and parts into different new positions. For example imagine the post box walking, writing and posting the letter. Try writing a children's story about it. Practise other similar exercises, in other areas – catching a train or walking to the station. Here you might see the train or engine walking, or the ticket-controller pulling the train. Play the game as a fun phantasy activity, but it is also valuable in helping to loosen up rigid ideas, to see component parts and to stimulate greater imaginative thought in everyday situations.

2. The unusual, alternative and non-conventional are often also the creative. Try to break-down your patterns, controls and rules, the way you see and relate to others and new situations. Don't think and perceive how *others* want you to, but be an authentic individual, different and original in your approach to every aspect of life. Everyone has creative gifts within them. Set these in motion by mobilising courage, determination and energy. Begin to look more honestly at yourself, to see why and where your creativity has become negated by ritual, convention, routine and habit.

3. Patterns, convention, tradition and habit are all forms of pressure. Such impositions usually aim to re-instate and re-confirm the past. The pressures can be subtle so that you are unaware of them at a cost to originality.

4. Look more closely at your daily work and activity programmes, leisure and comfort patterns. See if these follow the same routines day after day without significant alteration. Retrace your most predictable behaviour patterns and try to understand why they exist at all. Clarify habits, rituals and motivations for each particular set pattern, also the limitations of such routines. Next try to vary them as much as possible. The reason is not just change, but to give an opportunity for alternatives, new, better ways – even for daily routine and chores. In this way you will slowly become more open and less restricted by mundane patterns, able to express alternatives with more time for new

different areas. It may be possible to walk home from the office by a different route, or to drive back through the country, either earlier or a little later. You may find the journey takes 10-15 minutes longer, yet still gain time by not having to unwind for an hour after work. A colleague working in Cambridge drove there from Surrey each week to arrive by 9.00 a.m. He automatically assumed that a car was cheapest, fastest and most practical way to travel. Only when forced to consider alternatives because the car was garaged, did he in fact find that the journey by train was cheaper and almost as fast. It was also less tiring so that he relaxed more, at the end of the day was less tired and achieved more overall with a significant reduction in stress.

5. Try changing your environment so that new perspectives develop. Get away from established work patterns and place-domination. Consider working from home instead of the office for one day a week. If this is not possible work outside in the garden or country. Take a portable table, chair, note-book or typewriter. Work and record in the new environment and note how usual problems seem less important and intrusive. If this does not work for you, or is impossible and unrealistic, question if you are quite sure it cannot be done, then look for ways to make it a reality. Find different ways to be less of a slave to environment and routine. See where and how you are blocked and then how to change or modify it. Getting away from usual office confines may not solve everything, but

free you just sufficiently to gain insight and perspective into blocks. There are no 'wrongs' in creative thinking, only attempts to express, practise and experiment. Aim for new ways of looking and thinking within existing areas of activity. Self-judgement or self-criticism should not enter into it, or be a factor, except one to overcome. Consider changes, moves, juxta-positions and alternatives, to see new outcomes and stepping-stones to other realities, to a new you – and one which is more fulfilled.

6. Where there is constant friction, resentment or irritability in the home or office, an emotional or a stalemate situation, distance yourself for a time from the situation. Consider a weekend break or a different forum of dis-cussion – a working brunch perhaps, or a different restaurant. Get outside the usual routines of a problem area. This is necessary because we all make fixed associations about others and often only a radical change of situation and venue helps attitudes to change. We behave differently at home, from in the office, with colleagues or when under scrutiny. Getting out of environment routine is essential to break away from fixed patterns and unsolveable situations.

7. Where there is a problem of any kind, try to break it down to basics. Like a child with a toy or game, dismantle it and see the areas where there is most difficulty and where it is minimal. Be even more like a child with a game when trying to creatively solve the problem. Dis-mantle, re-build, form new shapes and ideas for

new and different end-results. Practise this in phantasy situations as well as reality ones. Practise breaking-down and re-forming the component-elements in existing pressure areas and be as relaxed and 'at play' when you are in the actual situation.

8. Free the simplest everyday experiences, like brushing your teeth, waking up, eating breakfast into their basic parts.
Brushing your teeth may contain
1. Waking with a dry mouth.
2. A sense of discomfort.
3. Desire for freshness.
4. Recall of the feeling of a clean, cool, fresh mouth.
5. The act of brushing your teeth.
6. The sense of freshness and cool moisture.
7. Desire to eat an apple, have breakfast or drink some tea.

9. Let the mind run free, associating to ideas as they occur without inhibition, judgement or explanation. However phantastic, unreal the images, ideas and thoughts, just experience them as they occur. See such images as the waves of a sea of creative potential within you arriving on shores of sensitivity and awareness. These associations have value because they relax and free you from the necessity to explain, understand or find immediate answers. Let the images work for you, even when insistent and under emotional pressure. Look always for the

unusual as it comes up, the new perspective, because it is there if you will allow yourself to perceive it.

If there are no new ideas or inspirations, then relax, be patient and allow anxiety, fear or stress-currents to lessen. These blind you to new openings by their very intensity and must be brought back into balance by practise, acceptance and relaxation.

10. Develop independence and separateness. Isolation may even be positive where a job, relationship or routine is negative or stultifying. Separation provides a space within a relationship or family situation, especially where it has become negative and confining. In this way you may also break with passivity, conditioning, fear and patterned behaviour so that a more real, creative authentic you emerges.

Practise separating from rigid routines of behaviour, belief, dogma and doctrine which you have accumulated over the years, however sacred. Questioning and doubts in an area of commitment are quite healthy and permissible. Re-think your convictions and beliefs, where you are committed – in a personal, political or religious way. Once you have done this, stand back, and ascertain whether such beliefs and convictions still accurately reflect you now. Make sure that they are not areas of reassurance and addiction, like a food or drink habit, a comforting routine only which limits change and growth.

11. Separate yourself from habit and routine. Comfort, security and routine, at a cost to personal integrity and creativity, is always negative, building-up resentment and ill-health as well as destroying achievement potential and creative personal development.

A woman seen in consultation for severe obesity also had an arthritic knee problem. She prepared meals daily for her invalid mother. There were severe stress problems at home because she never took a holiday or saw friends, unable to leave mother or make alternative arrangements. When a health crisis occurred her mother was put in a nursing home and she was obliged to separate more. New openings and contacts for both daughter and mother developed as a result with a new determination to slim for my patient. All of this could have happened years before and the illness was only the final expression of pent-up tension and anxiety. It could have been prevented if the excessive dependency routine had been seen and resolved earlier.

12. Articulate, challenge, overturn and reverse your own opinions as much as those of others. Phantasise, to stimulate greater breadths of ideas, sensitivity and awareness. In this way oppose shyness, self-consciousness and any tendency to withold. Let yourself range in the

widest sense of the word. In this way you can make apparently threatening, strange, inhibiting situations more ordinary and part of everyday life. Aim to move, talk, visit and to see in as many different ways as possible, especially if you have any tendency to be withdrawn or introverted.

If you are never still, always on the move, too active, aim to talk less and listen more, to be quiet and to find yourself in stillness. Finding yourself, you will also find new awareness, new perspectives and new solutions. Still the rushing activity and find out who you are as much as what you need. Once you are clearer about the real goals then start to activate them today rather than tomorrow.

13. Try a new area of interest which you have always wanted to attempt – for example painting, photography, swimming, pottery, music or a sport. Look with new perception, as yourself, and not as others have made you or want you to be. Look, for new thinking and new perceptions as you develop new interests, new feelings and new ideas. Be more daring with more audacity. Take a chance and be prepared to expose yourself, to make mistakes, but begin now.

14. Implement delayed plans and ideas for the future. Begin again in new and different ways, with new determination, and interest. In this way you will become different. By looking, and thinking differently, you will be different. We

are not only what we think but also what we see and perceive. Try now, not later with the things you have always wanted to achieve. Don't put off plans until tomorrow. It is nearly always a mistake to delay and often a defence. See plans in some ways as a delaying tactic to put off involvement, exposure and commitment today. The future is still tomorrow and in many ways the unknown. Now is now, as it is happening. Don't be put off by projects and promises, what you will do when 'the time is right', have the money or your health is better. Activate tomorrow's plans today. Overturn unconscious intentions to never really put them into action. None of us know what tomorrow's world will be. Action now, not later is a password to growth and the way to free yourself from promises and delaying uninvolvement.

15. Aim each day to make the improbable probable, the impossible possible. At every level, question the unquestionable, especially the clichés, labels and assumptions you are using that something cannot be done because it is 'not the moment' or you are 'too old'. Challenge every label and hunt them out within yourself. Listen much more as you talk and speak. Have fun by confronting and reversing your own clichés and be amazed at what you will achieve, enjoy and accomplish.

16. Depth and sensitivity are constantly whittled away by the increased use of gadgetry we are told we must buy. If they truly liberate time and leisure, cut down on uncreative chores

– then this is an advance. But use the gadgets and don't let them run you. A computer, like a calculator, is a useful tool, but not always a necessity. Often it has severe limitations and disadvantages. The major danger of the gadget is that it takes over to the exclusion of all else. When using it, be quite sure you are not addicted or dependent upon it, paralysing thought, action or initiative. Understand the principles and fundamentals of each gadget whenever possible. If possible adjust and repair it when there is a problem. Consider ways to improve or expand the gadgets you are using and if you have a new original idea, patent it so that it becomes a reality-achievement.

An automatic gear-box may be an advantage in traffic, but less stimulating or interesting in the country or highway because it limits personal driving control and expression. Always make the gadget serve and act as a stimulus to new thinking and learning, releasing time and energy, in the service of freeing you rather than as an object for a captive market.

17. In general practise less rather than greater control to be more spontaneous and original. But 'blowing off steam' and outbursts of anger may be positive as long as they are freeing attempts to break through controls and personal limitations. Letting go is usually better than holding or damming-back. Even loss of control can be good if it helps positively break with self-destructive patterns. A lifetime of control, passivity, dependency and inhibition

may sometimes require a violent outburst in order to make the break, but not always. In general it is better to provoke rather than to be provoked but what matters is that either leads to changes in perception and understanding. Wrong, mistaken actions and expressions can often lead to new insight and learning. In general keep a balance, not controlled or controlling, nor 'thrown' emotionally by a new situation or happening.

18. Practise staying yourself, more centred, psychologically, less of a pawn for others to manipulate according to their needs, rather than your own. Manipulation is common – both at personal and media levels. Stay critical and you, guarding your judgement and your individuality. Practise finding loopholes in the labels and commercial promises. In this way you will become less easily influenced, less manipulated and more able to stay yourself until *you* decide, not others for you.

19. A sense of wonder, simplicity of response and the ability to be moved by simple things is a wonderful thing. The spontaneity and naturalness of the healthy young child is striking until he or she is contaminated and to some extent destroyed by educators, upbringing and society. Try to see and feel yourself as a child again. Recall your earliest interests, enthusiasms, ideas and dramas. See yourself again as you were then. If necessary stimulate recall by looking at photographs.

Try consciously to regress – to feel yourself the child again. Re-experience earlier urges, drives, passions and enthusiasms. See how and when you lost them and whether this followed a hurt, 'event' or trauma. Recapture frequently this lost child you and on each occasion let yourself feel the child, replenished, rejuvenated and renewed.

20. Look more closely at routines, rituals, attitudes and ways of behaving. If necessary keep a note-book to record them clearly. They are important, mainly unconscious, and matter because they tie you down to patterns and mediocrity, blocking both change and response to challenge. Routines limit you imaginatively lessening the fullness of your individuality. Practise changes in routine, however convenient, comfortable and logical they have become. Make some changes and experiment with new, wider contacts, exposures and experiences. If you use a bus or tram, consider walking or a bicycle. Consider alternative routes, way of travel, walking, the train or coach on some days of the week. Experiment, try alternatives and don't make assumptions not based on experience.

21. Everyone needs a period of daily quiet for themselves so that they can enjoy relaxation and be themselves. During a busy working day, try to take at least three 5 minute periods of relaxation to be still and quiet. During these times, relax the whole body. Let thoughts and ideas come up into your mind as they happen.

Don't shut them out, but don't be affected or influenced by them either. Relax both body and mind, the thoughts unfixed, flexible, aware, easy, but not soporific or asleep. During these times, try not to think about specific problems, just be still and unperturbed. Whenever a new thought, insight or understanding develops, write it down whilst remaining relaxed. Practise this daily.

22. Meditation can be valuable and differs from relaxation in that the mind is more concentrated on a particular area to the exclusion of other ideas encouraging greater depths of self-awareness and realisation. When meditation is kept imaginative and undogmatic, it is freeing, but it is important to keep it so and not part of a rigid routine or a meaningless pattern. In general, meditation facilitates contact with the deepest aspects of self, the life force and inspirational depths. Meditation must be regular and for a period of at least 20 minutes daily, part of a regular attempt to reach greater awareness. It relaxes deeply, reducing tension, and can be a significant aid to creative insight and self-knowledge.

23. Practise visualisation as regularly as relaxation or meditation, seeing the end-result so clearly that you can touch, smell, feel and make use of, if necessary. Feel the visual image as part of you and a *fait accompli* without doubt, fear, uncertainty, or negative thought of any kind.

When you visualise, always fragment the component parts, reversing imagery and relocate the colours. Use them to create new different ideas for fun, flexibility and pleasure.

24. Encourage 'other' alternative solutions, however illogical or impossible to be tried and expressed. It is essential to accept and tolerate a certain mystery in life, a certain aspect of belief without knowing. Accept the creative force as intrinsic drive, derived directly from the inspirational-creative and fundamental to all life. You cannot always know – in the sense of being able to formulate, intellectualise, control, explain or define every phenomena, because defining is itself a limitation and a brake to the free-flow of creativity. Accept some degree of mystery, of not being in control, of not-knowing, accepting some things as they are without definition and explanation. In this way, there is less danger of limiting and confining perception to self-satisfying explanations, established boundaries and man-made limits.

25. Try to visualise the mystery of a creative universe and creative force which is all-pervading. Feel yourself part of a greater mosaic than the one you usually imagine, with its narrow patterns of self-interest. Create and visualise a universal creative energy or substance and see as yourself as part of it, expressing yourself through the ultimate mystery.

Even if the concept does not feel 'right', still try to imagine it. It may seem nonsensical, imaginative, or unscientific and unproveable. Nevertheless see yourself as an intrinsic part of a greater inspirational unity and in resonance with it. Feel its potential energy, greater breadths and universality. Try to feel this energy force, as a vital force within each part of you. Accept that it is largely unknown, unrecognised yet gives you access to the ultimates of time, space and achievement, if you will allow it. Realise how such potential can lead to unlimited creativeness and renewal. See the creative energy force as timeless, with links back to all man's experience and wisdom from past and future. Practise regular contact and visualisation at this level. Let go of the limitations of logic and reason for this exercise.

26. Be 'on the ready' with pen and note-book, especially at night, so that half-formulated ideas and jottings can be recorded as they occur. Note key words, partial ideas and associations, to be used later in creative work and ideas-development. Type these mental jottings if possible and elaborate and associate to them as you record. Fill any gaps in the associations later, however wild or improbable, developing promising ideas as they occur.

See them as parts of ideas, development and associations, in a partial, unelaborated form and in this way more valuable. Use different coloured inks when recording different sections – dreams or insights related to a specific problem. Create a theme or story with these thought-elements as you record them. Think of them as developing potential solutions to a challenge. How often have you said with hindsight – why didn't I see it before? it was there all the time 'staring me in the face'. Find solutions, answers and insights within your jottings-book in the now.

Develop a completely new thought theme with your recorded part-ideas as well as a variety of solutions in contrast to your usual thinking. Note day as well as night dreams, especially if suddenly recalled or fleeting. See such notes as ideas – sketches for new development, bricks to other ideas and expressions. Make your notes as clear and coherent as possible; if not, you may find them incomprehensible later, because of unconscious opposition to change and recall. Be as clear as possible at the time and enlarge each note afterwards with other associations and ideas.

27. In general, listen to nature and stay as close to natural things as possible. Be aware of time, changes, the seasons, natural rhythms, including your own personal ones. Whenever you are walking, listen and look. Rise at different times of day, earlier in the summer, later in the winter. Look at the sun-rise and sun-set, learn to be still, in contact yet a part of nature.

28. At all times aim to be free, to expand, to develop yourself, both ideas and your essential individuality to a maximum. Do this in the

broadest, most imaginative, pleasant and enjoyable way possible. Minimise stress and intrusion at all times. Free yourself whenever possible of limiting factors, particularly negative pressures. Find insight and understanding within yourself as much as intrinsic wisdom and potential. Make contacts, giving-out to enrich and give experience to others, but avoid being controlled, manipulated, used or fettered to your own loss. Try to resolve psychological inhibitions and blocks. These have roots in infancy. Creativity should not be dominated by repetitive immature phantasies and fears as these are self-destructive. Limiting and self-perpetuating, they act only in their own interest and should be confronted as soon as possible because of their self-limiting actions and their opposition to change and growth.

29. Use dreams creatively for new thought development. Whenever possible think through them the same day. Let dreams work for you and be a significant part of problem-solving because of their close proximity to the unconscious. Dream language should be intuitively sensed, like poetry or a painting. Don't always seek intellectual understanding because if you do, you will only impose your own limitations. It is more valuable is to use the spontaneous associations of feelings, associations and memories that occur. Don't expect direct answers to problems. This can occur but it is rare and much more you should look for new insights, new approaches and perceptions to old problems. Dream language is

symbolic and usually unpolluted by education
or upbringing and in this way it has a great deal
to offer for the creative mind, to insight and
personal development.

Chapter fifteen

Further Recommendations for Personal Expansion and Growth

1. Stop seeing the faults and shortcomings of others.

2. Start admitting their positive sides too .

3. Acknowledge more your own faults and limitations but also acknowledge your strengths.

4. Stop looking backwards all the time and begin to look forward also.

5. In general, think less and do more.

6. Talk less and listen more.

7. Give out more to others.

8. Avoid dogma of your own making and that of others, especially where dialogue or

discussion are negative, unnecessary and undesirable.

9. Stop repeating yourself – both in words as well as thoughts.

10. Stop exploiting others, either people or animals.

11. Experience life with more respect, reverence and love.

12. Be aware of your limitations and life-span.

13. Stop being omnipotent and playing God.

14. Avoid addictions, dependency of any kind, especially food, alcohol, people, drugs and social props.

15. Treat everything and everyone with sensitivity, care, thoughtfulness and discretion.

16. Remember the inter-dependence of all life and all creatures.

17. Beware of false Saints, Seers and Educationalists.

18. Avoid obsessional-rigid thinking.

19. Expand and develop throughout life for health, life and the expression of the creative-inspirational force.

20. Limit stress to a minimum. You cannot avoid it totally but don't let it control you, rather let it work for you.

Where there is a relationship problem, see your own contribution, how you aggravate it and create uncertainty or tension. See where you can give more and alter the situation. Stop criticising others and give more so that the creative self can expand and bring perspective and balance.

In general, it is pointless and negative to see faults in others, stultifying and uncreative. It is a cause of resentment, counter-reaction and sense of rejection so that a psychological impasse is created that neither can easily resolve.

See what is now and look to this day. Stop looking back with regret, jealousy, hatred or resentment. Feel forgiveness, love and gratitude for the day, the year, the opportunity to express, the life-learning experiences. Be prepared to let go in order to more forward. Especially let go of old resentments, possessiveness, wounds, scars and hurts. Live more completely, totally and more involved. This will free you for tomorrow and with it there will be less impulse to look back, to retreat and withdraw.

Think less, in an intellectual, controlled sense and *feel* more with the intuitive-sensitive you. Listen to others, don't judge or pre-judge. Try to understand more and to demand less.

Don't jump immediately into a conversation unless you have something to say or contribute. Be spontaneous, but differentiate within yourself, negative impulsiveness, the need to hear your own voice and comments. A truly spontaneous, creative comment which relates to you now is expression without effort.

Be more forgiving and stop feeling that you have a private line to divine knowing. You have divinity and dignity, but not omnipotence and absolute certainty. If you feel quite certain about something immediately, the possibility is that you are acting on impulse to preserve the *status quo* and sameness, to block growth and change.

Avoid false saints, authorities, dictators or falling into the trap of becoming one yourself. Take time off, from the familiar patterns, routine, controls, and rigidity. Try to experience realities as they are, unfold and develop.

Limit any tendency to repeat yourself. Say it once only clearly, but don't fill valuable time and contact with a cacophony of repetition and attention-seeking platitudes as a block to learning, listening, feeling and growing. Think of others when you express yourself – they matter at least as much as you.

Pay less attention to the doctrinal, including politics, religion, or the family. They probably have little real meaning for you in terms of personal evolving. In general dogmas bind and fetter into a subdued state. Out-moded concepts also seek to confuse, manipulate and limit, having lost their simple original aims. In general be more aware, more present in the now, as you are, naturally yourself with others. Seek the simple, the undefined, the new, the evolving, the changing, the unknown, as opposed to the familiar and the comfortable. Dogma is for the benefit of institutions and has little to offer you in terms of understanding, and development because it is both absolute and static. Develop growth and awareness in the now, where you must be for new creative awareness to occur.

Anything that exploits or uses others, especially animals, cannot be defended and is out of harmony with nature and creativity. These should be avoided totally, not encouraged nor supported.

Don't gobble-up food as if filling a hole. You are a unique, dignified, loving, creative being. Allow the creative-inspirational to function on every occasion and don't stifle it by eating without appreciation and a sense of occasion. Realise the preparation of a meal, the stages, planning and cooking. Eat with more enjoyment, appreciation, reverence, thanks and eat slowly.

Try to understand the underlying message of every contact, its aims, fears and reality. Don't let others decide for you or influence you. Take decisions yourself and be captain of your own ship, taking responsibility for inevitable disasters, vicissitudes, happenings, successes and failures. Whenever others are pressurising you unduly, distance yourself for a time, to find yourself, to live life more slowly and to be still .

Remember the limitations of life span and the body cloak. Life is not infinite nor forever. You are *homo sapiens,* not omnipotent. Get on with life now, don't delay for one more day. Time is short, precious and on the wing. However much you may still have in store, too much has been wasted or used uncreatively. Avoid the trap of thinking that life is forever, it is not and one day you too will make a way for others, like those before. Start today being more you, more authentic, more in touch with the real you, more giving, more expanding and more caring.

Avoid being over-enthusiastic and over-excited, not even about your own new ideas or break-throughs into creativity. Remember that each is a stepping stone at best, something to be savoured, reflected upon, accepted or rejected but not something to get 'wild' over. Conserve enthusiasm, but not natural spontaneity, and don't over-value or idealise. In this way you will be less disappointed with yourself as much as with others.

We all need each other in some way and certainly 'no man is an island'. We must give out to learn. Doctors have as much to learn from their patients as to give to them and the same is true of parents with children. In general we grow by listening and doing. The path of listening is a difficult one but listen and learn we must, in order to be able to give out more of ourselves.

Avoid those with impressive volumes of imagery, metaphor, and oratory, seeking to entrap, control or influence you. In general the easy promise aims to paralyse and seduce judgement and discerning, limiting both creativity and individuality. Use caution with those who are part of a system and take little account of your individuality. Unless they support, help develop imaginative growth and originality in life, you are probably being lulled or programmed into passivity and uncreative credence.

Chapter sixteen

Creative Workshops

The notes and suggestions that follow are by way of recommendation and guide-line only, not definitive in any way.

Workshops are small group meetings aiming to extend the personal exercises and recommendations. It is suggested that each group consist of not more than twelve persons and meets weekly on the same day, at the same time for a period of eight or ten weeks.

Each workshop aims to free creative energy drives in their most frequent areas of blockage – physical as well as psychological, followed by meetings where creativity can develop and be expressed and experienced in the now.

The composition of each group should be varied at the discretion of the leader. Actual age, background and experience of members is less important than a well-balanced group. In general each group should stay with the same members throughout the workshops and not re-group for different sessions.

Physical Blocks to Creativity: (1 hour)

This should be the first meeting with the stated aim to discuss and correct physical factors that undermine, divert or impose physical factors upon your creative expression. Typical areas include diet, exercise, general health and specific problems. How best to correct or approach a physical problem. Bringing the individual back into physical balance. Progress reports and outcome can be discussed and should be encouraged. Prevention is the best medicine and could be a group theme. The effects of blocked creative drive and outlet may be expressed physically with symptoms of jaded fatigue, depletion, depression or lack of drive. Self-neglect in terms of diet and exercise might be considered, also posture, sleep, movement, relaxation, eating, alcohol, smoking and an approach to nutrition in general. The aim is to study and perceive new ways to improve health,to an optimum for each member, so that there is a more effective framework for inspirational expression rather than a limited, neglected or painful one.

Psychological Blocks to Creativity: (1 hour)

The aim of the second group is to focus on any patterns of psychological habit and defence blocking goal-achievement, personal expression, individuality and freedom to experiment, play and create. The task is not to analyse specific problems, but to focus on limitations of endeavour, personal expression and innovation: rigid attitudes, negative judgement, lack of sensitivity are blocks to self-expression. Lack of flexibility and openness may be another group consideration. As these emerge more clearly during discussion specific negative patterns and blocks can be more clearly seen.

Creative thinking is lost or diverted by low self-esteem, inward-directed attitudes, hopelessness, despair, depression and loss of confidence. Behaviour patterns are important, especially when these are destructive and limiting, preserved for familiarity and safety. Such defences undermine security and limit aspects of the self already built-up. Develop psychological awareness by new reality experiences especially feeling, discussion and sharing.

Reduce fear, phantasy-assumption, conviction and ritual by open discussion. Avoid secrets, shame and guilt by confrontation and sharing. Try to see changes as they occur in reality as well as internally and psychologically as the group grows and matures. The group may play a role in reducing tension and stress.

Creative Freedom: (1 1/2 hours)

The third group aims for a tangible discussion and verbalisation of what has been freed by the previous groups. It should begin after a short break of 15 - 30 minutes follow the psychological group. Start with a period of quiet, meditation and repose to find a theme which can be developed and allowed to grow. This workshop should be different from the preceding ones, emphasising different ideas, creative phantasy and new perceptions. Anything new, seen, felt or conceived during the week should be allowed to emerge and be shared, even if a half-formed, partial idea, direction or 'hunch'. An experience might be hearing a first cuckoo, being moved to tears, the smell of a spring flower, a painting, tears or change within a relationship. In general give closest attention to areas that have moved or evolved and are a stimulus to new feelings and interest, a sense of awe, wonder or admiration. 'Breakthrough' ideas with links and repercussions in other areas are important in the change, resolution and resolving of stalemate situations.

Creativity Now: (1 1/2 hours)

Using brainstorming principles, the group choses its own task for the session and then quite freely verbalises and associates to it. Each suggestion which emerges is recorded, however seemingly impossible, unreal or fantastic, without using logical or critical judgement.

The purpose is to stimulate a free-flow of new ideas, links, discussion, humour and perception of an actual problem. The results of the brainstorming which may last from 20-30 minutes are sifted and discussed. The group decides which new alternative or approach is most helpful and practical and most likely to evoke a different solution. Outcome is followed-up in subsequent groups.

Aim to record, describe and feel changes as they occur, in any field – work or play. Try to bring emerging, developing ideas into focus so that each person feels and experiences them, their potential energy and drive.

The final workshops are the deepest and should be the most spontaneous and least organised ones in terms of leadership or direction. In this way it can become its own dynamo, teacher and stimulus from within, the actual leader present more as a support and observer. Always consider the outward, tangible, external expressions of the creative-inspirational as evidence of inner existence and the life-force.

New insights can be discussed within the group as to outcome and meaning. An attempt in difficult areas leads to experience, confidence and knowledge limiting the repetitive, uncreative, circular thinking of the past.

The workshop may decide to work in an area of specific blockage. Ultimately each group will decide its own identity, work, strengths and limitations and the most useful areas to expand creativity.

Blocks to creativity are likely to emerge as opposing 'difficult' areas, at the same time giving an opportunity for their resolution.

Groups or individuals may meet or organise themselves as informal workshops for personal back-up and discussion where this is thought desirable.

FURTHER READING

	Publisher	Date
Anderson. H.		
Creativity and its Cultivation	Harper & Row	1959
Barnes. K.		
The Creative Imagination	Allen & Unwin	1967
Cropley. A.		
Creativity	Longmans	1967
Gowan. J.		
Creativity – Its Educational Implications	John Wiley	1967
Harrison. A.		
Making & Thinking - A Study of Intelligent Activities	Harvester	1978
Jennings. S.		
Creative Therapy	Pitman	1975
Kagan. J.		
Creativity and Learning	Mifflin	1967
Koestler. A.		
The Act of Creation	Hutchinson	1967
May. R.		
The Courage to Create	Collins	1976
Morris. P.		
Imagery and Consciousness	Hampson	1983

Parnes. S.
A Source Book of
Creative Thinking   Scribner   1962

Richardson. A.
Mental Imagery   Routledge   1969

Rugg. H.
Imagination   Harper & Row   1963

Samuels. M.
Seeing with the Mind's Eye   Random House 1975

Shouksmith. G.
Intelligence, Creativity and
Cognitive Style   Batsford   1970

Torrance. P.
Torrance Test of
Creative Thinking   Personnel   1966

Vernon. P.
Creativity - Selected Readings   Penguin   1970

Warnock. M.
Imagination   Faber   1976

Willings. D.
The Creatively Gifted   Woodhead
                                  Faulkner   1980

INDEX